# SALESFORCE

# SIMPLIFIED

*A simple and precise guide for understanding and using Salesforce*

Ramanathan J

Cover designed by Ramanathan J

# Table of Contents

# INTRODUCTION

The purpose of any business or a company is to generate profits for the investors in the company by providing value for the customers through products or service.

Any organization has numerous functions that enable the company to deliver value to its customers. Finance function manages funds and budgets, Human Resources recruits, trains and manages employees, Operations handle the regular functioning of company activities.

Marketing and Sales function in a company ensures that a customer from any market is aware of and is willing to purchase company products or services. Marketing and Sales function generates revenue for the company and the organization's operational efficiency determines the overall profits.

Hence, Marketing and Sales is one of the most critical and indispensable function in any company. An effective and efficient marketing and sales department will ensure that an organization stays competitive and makes profit in its relevant market or industry.

In many organizations, marketing and sales activities are executed as a part of one discipline. Marketing teams identify new markets, segment markets as per various demographic criteria and execute various marketing campaigns. In other words, marketing teams prepare the ground in order to generate sales for the company's products or services.

Individuals in sales teams are allocated sales territories and targets. Sales professionals are required to achieve sales numbers for their company products or services in their respective sales territories.

As a result, sales professionals are on a constant pursuit to acquire leads, qualify these leads, explore for potential opportunities from these qualified leads and convert the opportunities into possible sales.

A marketing and sales department in any organization will create a huge amount of data when it functions over a period of time. Some of this data could be point of sales records, purchase orders, ecommerce transactions or sales contracts. This data could be stored in the form of database or spreadsheet records.

Other form of data in marketing and sales function could be more unstructured or unformatted in nature. This could include call logs with leads, meeting history with prospects, details of contacts associated with leads, activity or task details and so on.

Many of this data need not be present in a computer database or Excel spreadsheet. Instead, call history with a lead could be in a sales professional's smartphone.

Similarly, request for information from a qualified lead could be inferred only from the email trail between sales team and the lead. As a result, a lot of unstructured data in a marketing and sales function is scattered across various sources in different formats.

Collective data generated by marketing and sales function could improve the overall efficiency and effectiveness of the department. Marketing and Sales professionals can extract compelling insights for increasing product sales and generating revenue by referring to a single source of data. This single source of data can eventually become a part of institutional memory in an organization. As a result, crucial information about markets or customers is not lost whenever sales professionals leave to join other organizations.

**Introducing Salesforce:** Salesforce is a customer relationship management (CRM) software solution that provides holistic view of a customer from various perspectives such as marketing, sales, and service. A typical CRM product enables users to store customer related information such as name, address, phone numbers as well as other activity data such as phone calls, emails, meetings and so on.

Salesforce CRM actively tracks and manages customer information. Users can send email to customers and track responses from the Salesforce platform itself. Salesforce empowers users to move on from manual and cumbersome processes so that they can effectively find more leads, finalize more deals and grow their business.

Salesforce as a single repository of customer information allows sales teams to engage their potential customers with personalized and relevant conversations. This eventually results in more sales revenue, increased returns on marketing campaigns and higher customer satisfaction.

**Salesforce as a cloud based solution:** Salesforce offers CRM solutions using cloud-computing based model. Cloud computing model allows applications to be delivered over the internet. As a result, cloud based applications can be run on any web browser. Cloud based applications also do not require any specific hardware or software to be installed on any computer.

Since Salesforce CRM solutions are available on the cloud, there is no need for customers to deploy expensive on premise IT staff for dedicated maintenance and support. Similarly, there is no need for expensive repairs, downtime or software upgrades with Salesforce CRM.

Cloud-computing model based Salesforce CRM solution empowers customers to scale and customize the product as per their requirement. Salesforce can cater to the need of small businesses, medium sized companies or large scale enterprises.

Salesforce is immediately available for customers to use in online, offline and mobile modes. Ease of use also enables widespread adoption of Salesforce among users.

# GETTING STARTED

We can access any of Salesforce's Sales, Marketing or Service cloud by subscribing on a USD per user and per month pricing model. We can subscribe to Salesforce Essentials, Professional, Enterprise or Unlimited editions according to the pricing model that we select. Salesforce Professional, Enterprise and Unlimited editions offer additional features such as lead registration and scoring, collaborative forecasting as well as workflow and approval automation.

You can also try the 30 day free trial to explore Salesforce platform and its various features. You will be required to sign up in the Salesforce free trial registration page before you can access the 30-day free trial version. You can enter the key words "Salesforce free trial" in Google and click on the Salesforce.com page for 30 day free trial to register your details or you can enter this link in your browser: (https://www.salesforce.com/in/form/signup/freetrial-industry-insurance/)

We will be using the 30 day free trial version for Salesforce in this guide.

Following screenshot displays the registration page for the Salesforce 30 day free trial version:

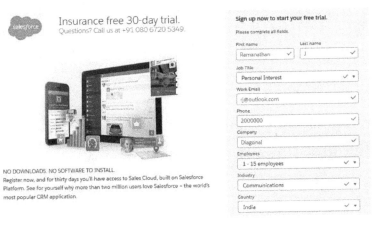

We can start to access Salesforce trial version on cloud once we verify our account from the email that we will receive from Salesforce.

The verification email from Salesforce would also include the login URL for accessing the platform. The email would also include the user name for accessing Salesforce. We will be accessing Salesforce using the URL (https://login.salesforce.com/).

Following is the login page for Salesforce:

We can set our password once we login from the above URL for the first time. We can subsequently access the Salesforce Home page.

**Home Page:** Salesforce Home page is the initial landing page when we login. Following image displays the Salesforce Home page:

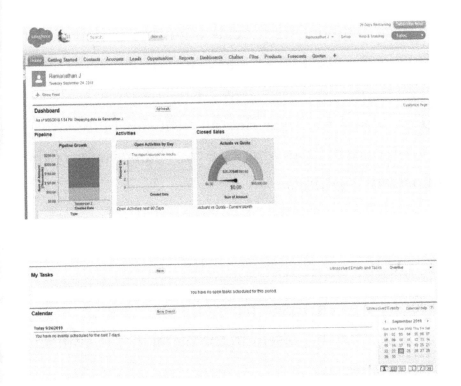

We can observe that the default Home page in Salesforce includes a Dashboard component with visualizations for Pipeline, Activities and Closed Sales as well as components for My Tasks and Calendar.

We can customize the Home page to view the components as per our requirements.

Home page components provide a quick overview about the key metrics and tasks for any user.

**User Profile and Settings:** The top right side of the Home page comprises of links where we can change some of the administrative settings.

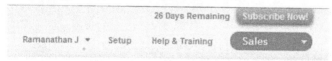

**My Profile:** We can access our profile by clicking on My Profile link which is present in the menu that is available with user name:

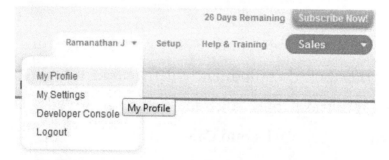

We can add our picture or edit our email ID in My Profile. This page also comprises of two tabs namely Feed and Overview.

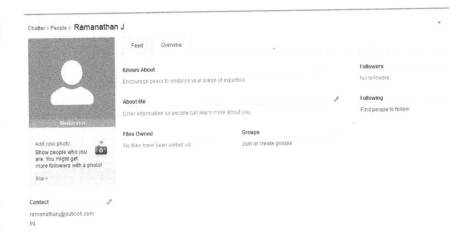

We can include more information about our self in the About Me section in the Overview tab of My Profile. We can do so by clicking on the Pencil icon present on the right side of About Me section.

Subsequent screen for Edit Profile comprises of two tabs namely About and Contact. We can include details about name, title, manage and other information about our self in the About tab of Edit Profile screen.

Similarly, we can enter our contact details such as phone number, email ID, street address, city, province and so on in the Contact tab of the Edit Profile screen.

We can click on Save All button to save changes made to our profile. These changes will be subsequently reflected in the My Profile page.

The Overview tab in the My Profile page also comprises of Files Owned, Groups, Followers and Following sections. We can create groups or join existing ones by clicking on the Join & create groups link in the Groups section. These groups could comprise of Salesforce users from the Sales and Marketing teams or employees from other departments in the organization.

Similarly, we can know more about our followers, who are also Salesforce users, from the Followers section in the Overview tab of My Profile page. We can follow other Salesforce users by clicking on Find people to follow link in the Following section to search for other users to follow.

In the subsequent screen, we can select the appropriate users and click on the Follow button to follow them.

All People

Once we start following a user, we can the user details in the Following section of My Profile page.

The Feed section in My Profile page provides a platform for Salesforce users to create posts, upload files, share links or create polls for their followers. Similarly, whenever we make changes to our profile settings in the

My Profile page, these updates are reflected as posts in the Feed section.

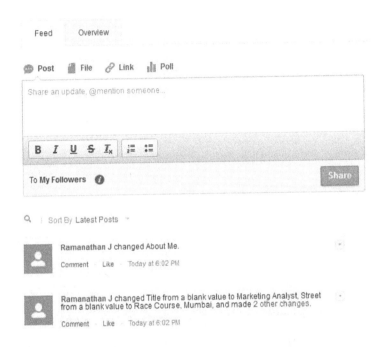

We can also mention other Salesforce users in our posts. Our followers within the Salesforce platform can comment or like on our posts.

A Contribution section located in the bottom left side of the My Profile page shows our total posts and comments, number of comments that we have received and the likes we have got so far.

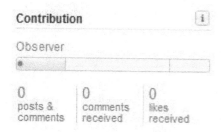

**Contribution**

Observer

| 0 | 0 | 0 |
|---|---|---|
| posts & comments | comments received | likes received |

If we observe the top left side of the My Profile page below the tabs pane, we will notice the following hierarchy:

Chatter › People › **Ramanathan J**

My Profile settings, posts, links, files and polls details are available in Chatter. Chatter is a Salesforce specific social media like platform. We can enter posts or follow users from Chatter or the My Profile page.

We can also add topics to our posts in order to make these posts popular among our followers. In other words, Chatter is a Facebook or Twitter like solution that is available within the Salesforce platform. Chatter is useful to initiate an informal conversations and to directly exchange ideas among various Salesforce users who could be following each other.

We can access Chatter by clicking on the Chatter link in the hierarchy displayed in the top right side of My Profile page or by clicking on the Chatter link in the tab section.

Following image displays the Chatter Home page when we click on the respective link:

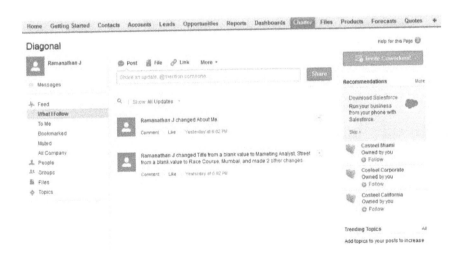

We can also bookmark certain posts or mute any feed items from the Chatter home page.

**My Settings:** We can access My Settings from the drop down menu that is present with our user name on the top right side of the screen.

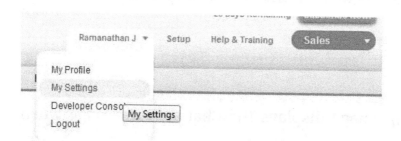

Following screenshot displays the My Settings page:

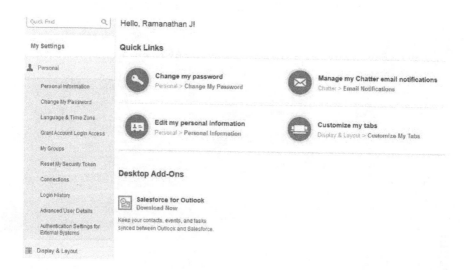

Following are some of the activities that we can complete from the My Settings page:

1. Change personal information such as username, password, name, email, address, language, time zone etc.

2. Alter display and layout by customizing tabs or pages.

3. Select if we want to view the social media profiles for our contacts, accounts or leads directly in Salesforce.

4. Set email name, address and signature.

5. Create new email templates or edit existing ones. You can create email templates for various purposes or activities as per your requirement.

6. View details of mass emails sent from your organization.

7. View or edit settings in My email to Salesforce feature. Emails are saved as activities in Salesforce against the respective records through settings that are stored in My email to Salesforce feature.

8. Edit Chatter feed and email notification settings.

9. Enable Calendar sharing with other Salesforce users or groups.

10. Edit Activity Reminder settings.

11. Import bulk data using Data Import Wizard.

**Setup Screen:** We can access the Setup page by clicking on the link present on the top right hand side of the screen or any Salesforce page.

Following screenshot displays the Setup page:

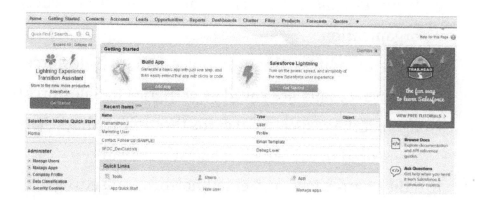

Some of the activities that we can perform from the Setup screen include administration tasks, customization of various tabs or apps, custom components deployment, new apps development and so on.

**Manage Users:** The left side pane of the Setup page comprises of Administer, Build, Deploy, Monitor and Checkout sections.

We will now look into some of the activities within the Manage Users category of Administer section.

**Administer**

☑ **Manage Users**
    Users
    Mass Email Users
    Roles
    Permission Sets
    Profiles
    User Management Settings
    Public Groups
    Queues
    Login History
    Identity Verification History

One of the most common activities in Salesforce administration is to add new users and edit details of current users. We can do so by clicking on Users within the Manage Users category of Administer section.

Following page is displayed when we click on the Users link:

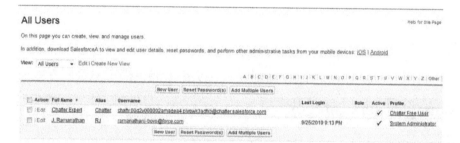

We can click on New User button to add a new user in the subsequent screen.

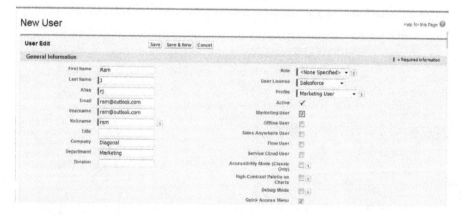

We can provide new user details such as name, email, username, role, user license and profile in this screen. Role and profile assignment for users will determine access to various apps and tabs.

We can click on Save button to store the new user details. If we are adding multiple users in sequence, we can click on Save & New button to store current user details and then immediately enter another user details in the New User details screen.

Following screen is displayed when we save new user detail:

Once we create a new user in Salesforce, the system will send an email to the new user in order to verify the change. This is to ensure system security.

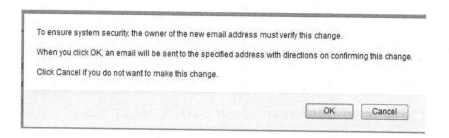

To ensure system security, the owner of the new email address must verify this change.

When you click OK, an email will be sent to the specified address with directions on confirming this change.

Click Cancel if you do not want to make this change.

OK       Cancel

The new user can check his email and click on the verification link to confirm the details.

**Role Hierarchy:** We can set up a role hierarchy to control how our team, department or organization accesses data within Salesforce.

Some of the typical role hierarchies include territory based, product based and company size based.

Role structure is determined on the basis of the sales territories controlled in territory based role hierarchy. For example, Executive VP Global Marketing and Sales in an organization could preside over VP Marketing and Sales for each sales territories namely, Eastern Region Sales, Western Region Sales and Northern Region Sales.

Product based role hierarchy establishes roles on the basis of various products and services offered by an organization. For example, an Executive VP Global Marketing and Sales could preside over VP Marketing and Sales for each product sold namely, Computer Hardware, Software and Network devices.

A user in a role hierarchy view and edit data as well as generate reports for all users below him in the hierarchy. However, the user will not be able to access data of users at the same level or those who are above him in the role hierarchy.

We can set up roles within Salesforce by clicking on Roles link within the Manage Users category of Administer section.

Following image displays the Role Hierarchy creation screen:

## Creating the Role Hierarchy

You can build on the existing role hierarchy shown on this page. To insert a new role, click **Add Role**.

**Your Organization's Role Hierarchy**

Collapse All Expand All

⊟ **Diagonal**

    ⌐·· Add Role

We can click on the Add Role link within the Role Hierarchy structure to set up new roles. Diagonal is the name of the sample organization in the above screenshot.

Following image displays the New Role creation screen:

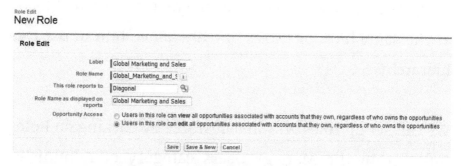

We are considering a product based role hierarchy for our example. In this case, the Global Marketing and Sales role will be at the top of hierarchy and will have complete access. We can click on Save button to store the newly created role details.

We can view the role details and can also assign users to this role in the subsequent screen. Following is the screenshot of the same:

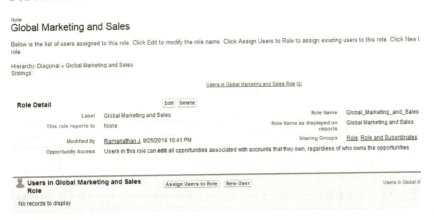

Role
Global Marketing and Sales

Below is the list of users assigned to this role. Click Edit to modify the role name. Click Assign Users to Role to assign existing users to this role. Click New U role.

Hierarchy: Diagonal » Global Marketing and Sales
Siblings:

Users in Global Marketing and Sales Role [0]

**Role Detail**                    Edit  Delete

Label    Global Marketing and Sales                   Role Name    Global_Marketing_and_Sales
This role reports to    None                 Role Name as displayed on    Global Marketing and Sales
                                                              reports
Modified By    Ramanathan J, 9/25/2019 10:41 PM      Sharing Groups    Role, Role and Subordinates
Opportunity Access    Users in this role can edit all opportunities associated with accounts that they own, regardless of who owns the opportunities

Users in Global Marketing and Sales         Assign Users to Role   New User                          Users in Global M
Role
No records to display

We can add users to the role by clicking on the Assign Users to Role button in the Role Detail screen.

We can search for available users and assign them to the respective roles in the subsequent screen. We can also remove current users from a role in this screen.

Following image displays the user assignment screen:

## Global Marketing and Sales

The users shown in the **Selected Users** list are currently assigned to the role **Global Marketing and Sales**.

To assign other users to this role:

- Make a selection from the drop-down list to show available users.
- Choose a user on the left and add them to the **Selected Users** list.

Removing a user from the **Selected Users** list deletes the role assignment for that user.

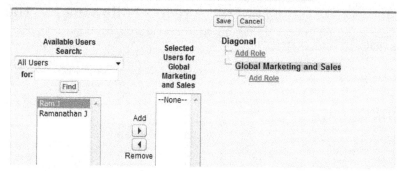

We can click on Save button to store the user assignment to role. We can now see the user details in the Role detail screen.

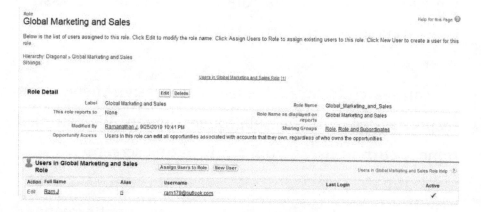

We can also assign users to roles from the Manage Users category in Administer section within the Setup page that we saw earlier. We can click on Users link within Manage Users and then click on Edit link for any user whom we want to assign to a role.

We can assign role to the selected user in the subsequent screen.

We can click on Save button to store the role details for the user.

We can create two other roles in our hierarchy namely Hardware Marketing and Sales as well as Software Marketing and Sales. These roles will relate to the Hardware products and Software products that are sold by our sample organization.

We can click on the Add Role link within the Global Marketing and Sales role to create new roles in the hierarchy.

## Creating the Role Hierarchy

You can build on the existing role hierarchy shown on this page. To insert a new role, click **Add Role**.

**Your Organization's Role Hierarchy**

Collapse All Expand All

⊟ **Diagonal**

   — Add Role

  ⊟ **Global Marketing and Sales**  Edit | Del | Assign

    Add Role

We will follow the steps mentioned earlier to create the new roles. We would also mention the role to which these newly created roles will report to. This will create the role hierarchy for the organization.

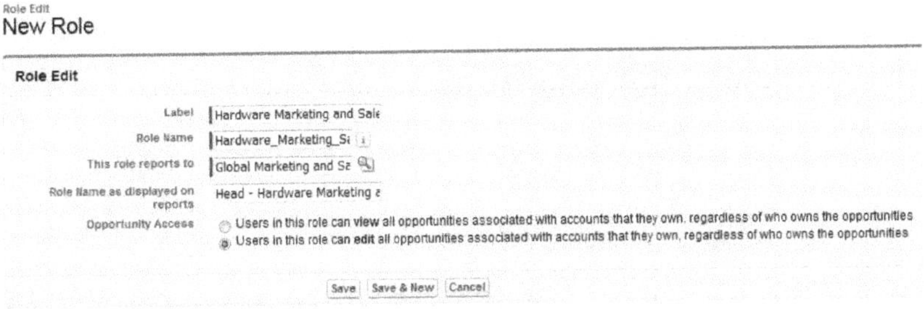

**Role Edit**

| | |
|---|---|
| Label | Hardware Marketing and Sale |
| Role Name | Hardware_Marketing_Si i |
| This role reports to | Global Marketing and Sa 🔍 |
| Role Name as displayed on reports | Head - Hardware Marketing a |
| Opportunity Access | ○ Users in this role can view all opportunities associated with accounts that they own, regardless of who owns the opportunities |
| | ◉ Users in this role can edit all opportunities associated with accounts that they own, regardless of who owns the opportunities |

[ Save ] [ Save & New ] [ Cancel ]

We can click on the Save & New button to store the current role details and to create the Software Marketing and Sales role in the subsequent screen.

The following image now displays the updated role hierarchy:

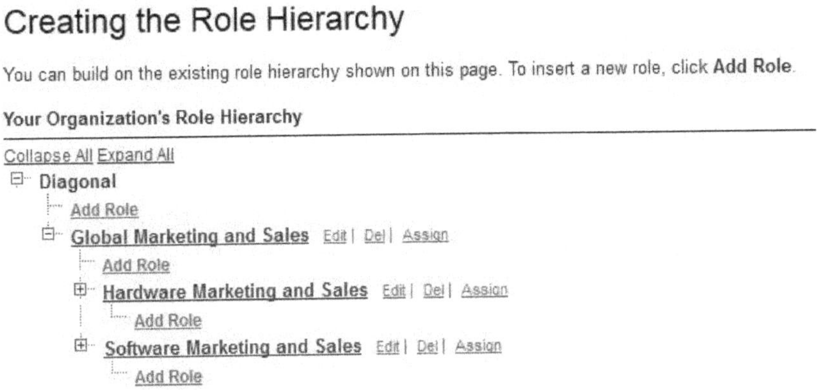

## Creating the Role Hierarchy

You can build on the existing role hierarchy shown on this page. To insert a new role, click **Add Role**.

**Your Organization's Role Hierarchy**

Collapse All Expand All
- Diagonal
  - Add Role
  - Global Marketing and Sales   Edit | Del | Assign
    - Add Role
    - Hardware Marketing and Sales   Edit | Del | Assign
      - Add Role
    - Software Marketing and Sales   Edit | Del | Assign
      - Add Role

The roles Hardware Marketing and Sales as well as Software Marketing and Sales are sibling roles because they occupy the same level in the overall role hierarchy.

In this way, we can create new roles in the hierarchy as per our organization's requirement.

**Profiles:** Any Salesforce instance is available with a set of standard user profiles. The list of user profiles can be accessed by clicking on Profiles link in the Manage Users category within the Administer section.

Following screenshot displays the list of user profiles:

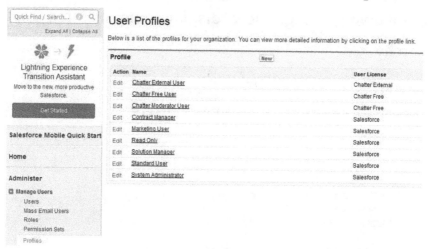

We can click on the Edit link for any existing user profile to change the current settings. We can set the default visibility settings for Apps and Tabs from the user profile edit screen. We can also edit password policies or session settings from the user profile edit screen. We can change the administrative permissions, general user permissions and standard object permissions for custom user profiles.

Following image displays the profile edit screen.

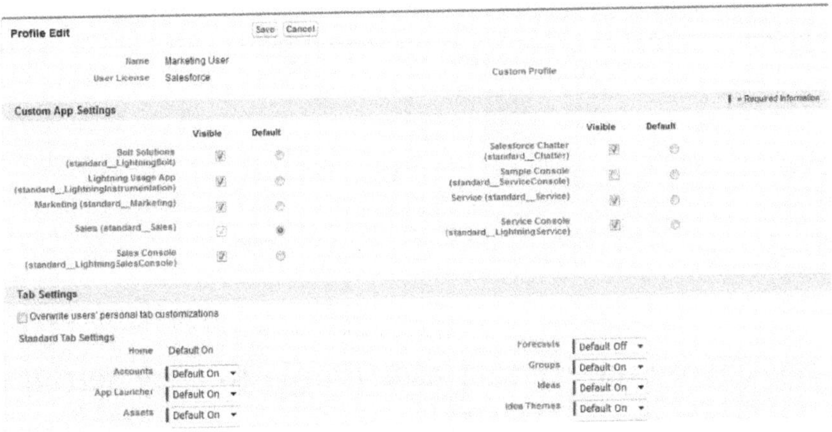

The standard tab settings values include Default On, Default Off and Tab Hidden. We can change the default visibility settings for any tab or app as per our requirement and then click on Save button to store the changes for the respective user profile.

We can click on the New button to create a new user profile. We must copy an existing user profile in order to create a new user profile. Following image displays the new user profile creation screen.

## Clone Profile

Enter the name of the new profile.

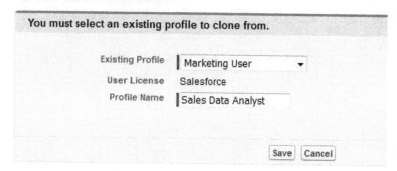

We can choose an existing user profile to copy settings from and provide a profile name for the new user profile. We can then click on the Save button to save the new user profile details.

The following screen shows the newly created user profile details:

## Sales Data Analyst

« Back to List: Users

Users with this profile have the permissions and page layouts listed below. Administrators can change a user's profile by editing that user's personal information.

If your organization uses Record Types, use the Edit links in the Record Type Settings section below to make one or more record types available to users with this profile.

Login IP Ranges [0] | Enabled Apex Class Access [0] | Enabled Visualforce Page Access [0] | Enabled External Data Source Access [0] | Enabled Named Credential Access [0] |
Enabled Service Presence Status Access [0] | Enabled Custom Permissions [0]

**Profile Detail**       Edit   Clone   Delete   View Users

| | | | |
|---|---|---|---|
| Name | Sales Data Analyst | Custom Profile | ✓ |
| User License | Salesforce | | |
| Description | | | |
| Created By | Ramanathan J, 9/26/2019 1:13 AM | Modified By | Ramanathan J, 9/26/2019 1:13 AM |

**Console Settings**

Console Layout    Sample Console  [ Edit ]

**Page Layouts**

| | | | |
|---|---|---|---|
| Global | Global Layout [ View Assignment ] | Opportunity | Opportunity Layout [ View Assignment ] |

We can click on the Edit button to change various options such as App settings, Tab settings, Administrative permissions, general user permissions and so on.

Following screenshot displays the custom user profile edit screen.

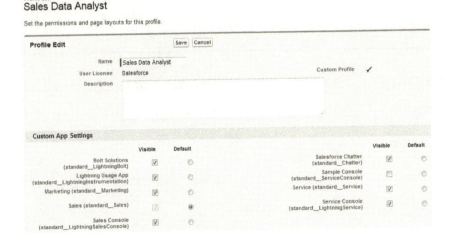

Profile Edit
## Sales Data Analyst

Set the permissions and page layouts for this profile.

**Profile Edit**       Save   Cancel

| | | | |
|---|---|---|---|
| Name | Sales Data Analyst | | |
| User License | Salesforce | Custom Profile | ✓ |
| Description | | | |

**Custom App Settings**

| | Visible | Default | | Visible | Default |
|---|---|---|---|---|---|
| Bolt Solutions (standard__LightningBolt) | ☑ | ○ | Salesforce Chatter (standard__Chatter) | ☑ | ○ |
| Lightning Usage App (standard__LightningInstrumentation) | ☑ | ○ | Sample Console (standard__ServiceConsole) | ☐ | ○ |
| Marketing (standard__Marketing) | ☑ | ○ | Service (standard__Service) | ☑ | ○ |
| Sales (standard__Sales) | ☑ | ◉ | Service Console (standard__LightningService) | ☑ | ○ |
| Sales Console (standard__LightningSalesConsole) | ☑ | ○ | | | |

**Apps and Tabs:** The top right side screen of any Salesforce page comprise of the App menu. Following image highlights the same:

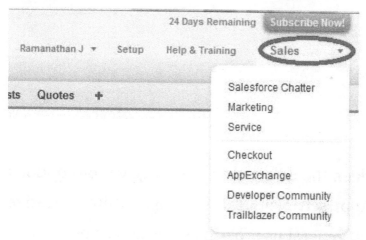

Sales, Marketing, Service and Chatter are some of the most commonly used apps in Salesforce. Each of these apps have a set of tabs that are visible by default. We can click on any of these apps from the menu to view the associated tabs.

For example, when we select the Sales option from the app menu, the following horizontal tab menu is displayed.

Similarly, when we select the Marketing option from the app menu, the following horizontal tab menu is displayed.

We can observe an additional tab titled Campaigns in the tab menu item for the Marketing app. Similarly, the Opportunities and Products tabs, that were visible by default for Sales app, are not visible now for the Marketing app.

When we select the Service option from the app menu, the following horizontal tab menu is displayed.

We can observe that Cases and Solutions tabs are now visible for the Service app.

**Customizing tab menu:** We can customize the tab menu by clicking on the plus icon that is present on the right side of the tab menu. Following screen is displayed when we click on this plus icon.

We can view all tabs in this screen. We can add tabs to the default display by clicking on the Customize My Tabs button on the right side of the page as shown above.

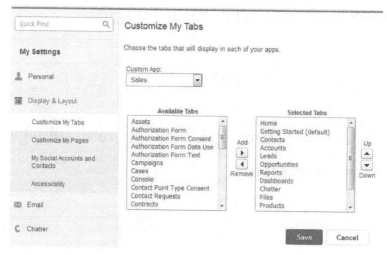

We can now select any app from the Custom App menu and then select the tabs that are to be displayed from the list of available tabs. We can remove any tabs, that we do not want to display, from the list of selected tabs. We can also alter the sequence in which the tabs are displayed by clicking on the Up or Down buttons.

We can also access the tab customization screen by clicking on the My Settings link in the context menu for user name on the top right hand side of the screen and then clicking on the Customize My Tabs option in the Display & Layout section on the left side pane.

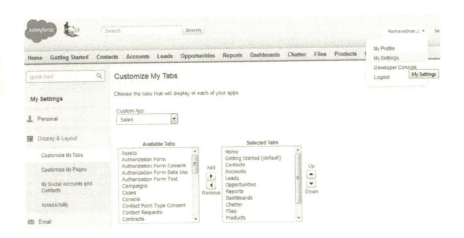

# SALES APP

# LEADS

We will now look into some of the core applications of Salesforce that empowers organizations to effectively manage their Sales and Marketing function. One of the core component in Salesforce is the Sales App which in turn comprises of various applications. Leads is one such application.

Leads application helps sales professionals in organizations to enter lead related data in Salesforce. Leads application also empowers users to update current Leads data in Salesforce whenever they interact or follow up with these Leads for exploring potential commercial opportunities. As sales professionals proceed further down the sales pipeline, the leads data can be subsequently transformed within Salesforce by associating the leads records with potential opportunities, accounts or contacts. Opportunities, accounts and contacts are other dedicated applications similar to Leads application within the Sales App component of Salesforce.

**Defining Leads:** A Lead can be any individual or company who could be possibly interested in doing business with our organization. In other words, a lead can be or can point to a potential purchaser of products and services from our company. We can use Leads data to follow up with sales queries and to approach new markets.

**Leads Home Page:** We can access the Leads application in Salesforce by clicking on Leads option in the horizontal tab menu.

Following image displays the Leads Home page when we click on the Leads option from the tab menu that is shown above.

The Leads home page comprises of various sections such as Recent Leads, Reports, Summary Reports and data editing tools.

The Recent Leads section in the Leads home page extracts data according to various views. Views display lead data according to our requirements. Some of the views that are available by default in Salesforce include Recently Viewed Leads, My Unread Leads and Recently Created Leads.

The top section of the Leads home page also comprises of a view drop down list. We can select any of the standard or custom views to view the lead data as per the view criteria.

Following image displays the View drop down list that is located on the top portion of the Lead home page.

Following is the lead data that is displayed when we select the All open leads option from the View drop down list.

We can select and edit any of the lead record from the data that is displayed for a view. We can change the status or owner or can add the lead record to a marketing campaign from the list of leads displayed in the view.

**Creating new lead:** We can create a new lead by clicking on the New button in the Recent Leads section of Leads home page.

We can also create a new lead by opening any view from the lead view drop down list and then clicking on the New Lead button in the subsequent screen.

Last name, company name and lead status are mandatory fields and hence we are required to enter information for these fields while creating a new lead. We can just enter the company name when we initially know the organization that we want to approach. We can enter the last name as NA or unknown for these cases.

We can enter the details for new lead and click on the Save button. Following image displays the new lead creation screen:

We can click on the Save & New button if we immediately want to enter details of a new lead after saving the current data.

Following image shows the portion of a page displayed after saving details of a new lead.

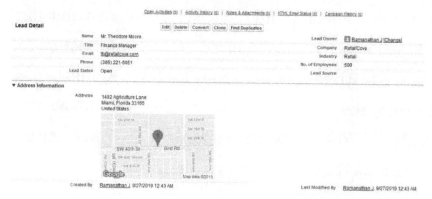

We can also keep a track of the open activities, activity history, any notes or attachments, email status and campaign history from the lead detail screen.

Following image shows the remaining portion of the lead detail page:

Custom Links

Google Maps

Edit | Delete | Convert | Clone | Find Duplicates

**Open Activities**                    New Task | New Event

No records to display

**Activity History**                   Log a Call | Mail Merge | Send an Email

No records to display

**Notes & Attachments**                New Note | Attach File

No records to display

**HTML Email Status**                  Send an Email

No records to display

**Campaign History**                   Add to Campaign

**Lead Status:** One of the key component of a standard lead process is to keep a track of lead status over a period of time. Often when we obtain a lead, we need to verify to ensure that there is a commercial or sales opportunity with the lead. For example, a lead must have a business requirement to purchase products from our company.

Secondly, a lead must have the necessary budget to do with our company.

Once we ensure that there is a definite commercial opportunity with an open lead, we can change the lead status to qualified. We can do so by editing any lead and changing the lead status to qualified.

Following image displays the lead detail edit screen:

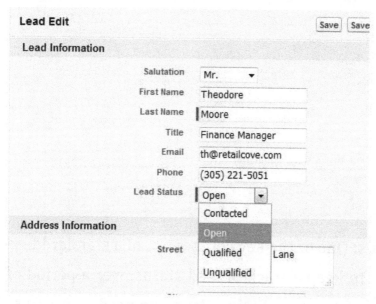

In case of our example, suppose our company sells software products. Our company's sales representative interacts with the lead Mr. Theodore whose details are mentioned in the above image and he comes to know that Theodore's finance team has a requirement and the budget to procure digital software solutions. In this case, we can qualify this lead by changing the Lead Status in the Lead Edit screen to Qualified. We can then click on Save button to store the details.

Following image shows the updated lead details screen.

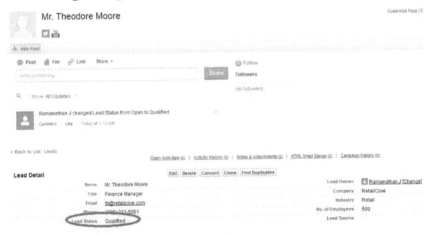

We can observe that there is a feed section where we can enter posts or links similar to a social media feed. When we edited the lead status in the previous step, a status update was automatically posted in the feed. We can hide this feed if we do not wish to post status updates by clicking on the Hide Feed button.

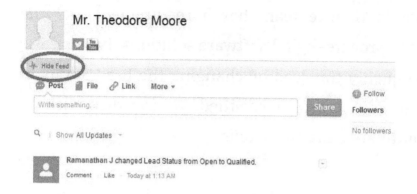

**Lead Source:** We can know a lead by meeting him/her in a trade show or seminar. We can also know about a lead by reading an advertisement. In this way, there are various ways by which we can identify a lead for potential commercial opportunity.

We can store details regarding how we came to know about any lead through the Lead Source field. We can enter this value when we create a new lead record or we can edit the current lead details.

Following image displays some of the values that are available by default in the lead source drop down list within the lead edit page.

We can select the appropriate value from the lead source drop down list and save the lead record.

**Cloning a lead:** We can sometimes come across multiple individuals, from a single company, who could be working across different departments in various designations. We can clone or copy the details of one lead to store details of other leads from the same company. In this case, we can just edit the key fields such as name, email, lead status or phone number whereas the rest of the details such as address or company name will remain the same.

For e.g. suppose our company develops software solutions for finance, HR and supply chain functions. Our sales representative attends a trade show where he meets Theodore, the finance manager from RetailCove whose details we saved as new lead earlier. Now our sales representative also meets Ms. Sheila Edwards in the same trade show. Sheila is the Director HR in RetailCove and hence she could be another lead to approach for commercial opportunities in HR software products.

We can clone a lead by performing the following steps:

1. Click on any of the links for leads in the Recent Leads section of the Leads home page or in any of the standard or custom Lead views.

| Recent Leads | New | |
|---|---|---|
| Name | | Company |
| Smith (Sample), Andy | | Universal Technologies |
| Moore, Theodore | | RetailCove |
| Gardner (Sample), John | | 3C Systems |
| Steele (Sample), Jim | | BigLife Inc. |

2. Click on the Clone button in the lead detail page.

3. Change the data in the necessary fields and save the new lead details.

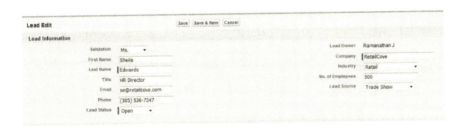

Thus, cloning option enables Salesforce users to quickly create new leads who could have similar attributes such as same company or department.

**Activity tracking with leads:** When a sales professional meets or comes to know about a lead initially, he will interact with the lead over a period of time to know more about the lead's business needs. In this way, the sales professional will be able to know about how his company's products or services could meet the lead's business requirements.

All interactions that takes place between a sales professional and any lead can be stored as activities for the lead. Let us consider our earlier example when our company's sales professional meets Ms. Sheila, who is the HR director with RetailCove, at a trade show. Subsequently, our sales representative interacts with Sheila in the following manner:

1. The sales representative calls Sheila and provides a brief introduction about the HR software solutions offered by his company.

2. Sheila expresses interest in some of the HR software products and asks the sales representative to send a detailed product brochure in an email.

3. The sales representative sends an email with product brochure as an attachment to Sheila.

4. The sales representative sends a follow up email to Sheila and requests time for meeting to demonstrate HR software product features.

We can track the series of steps listed for the above example in Salesforce from the lead detail page.

We can view the lead detail page by clicking on any lead listed in the Recent Leads section or in any lead view. Subsequently, we can observe the activity section for the respective lead in the lead detail page as displayed in the following image.

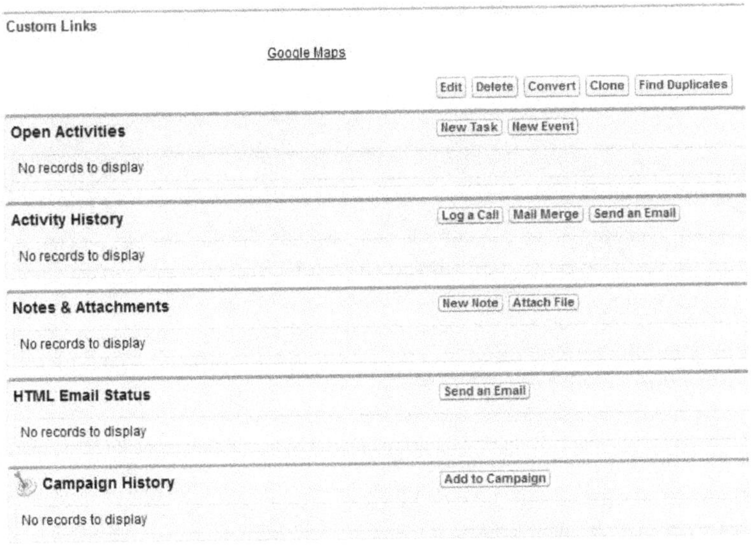

Custom Links

Google Maps

[ Edit ] [ Delete ] [ Convert ] [ Clone ] [ Find Duplicates ]

**Open Activities**                    [ New Task ] [ New Event ]

No records to display

**Activity History**                   [ Log a Call ] [ Mail Merge ] [ Send an Email ]

No records to display

**Notes & Attachments**                [ New Note ] [ Attach File ]

No records to display

**HTML Email Status**                  [ Send an Email ]

No records to display

**Campaign History**                   [ Add to Campaign ]

No records to display

**Creating new task:** We can create a new task for a lead by clicking on the New Task button in the Open Activities section within the lead detail page.

We can enter task details in the Task Edit screen when we click on the New Task button. We can consider our previous example and enter details for a call that we or need to make to Sheila soon to know more about her department's business requirements. Following image displays the Task Edit screen with the necessary details.

We can set the subject, task priority, comments, due date and task status in the Task Information section of the Task Edit screen.

We can also assign the task to any other Salesforce user from our team by selecting the respective user from the Assigned To field. For example, our company sales representative might be tracking multiple leads and hence he may want to assign this specific task to some other sales professional from his team. We can search for other Salesforce users by clicking on the lookup icon next to the Assigned To field in the Task Edit screen. Following images display the same:

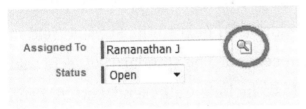

We can search for a single user or multiple users from a separate window when we click on the lookup icon next to the Assigned To field. We can select the users from the search results displayed in this window in order to assign them to a task.

Following image displays the lookup window for searching users.

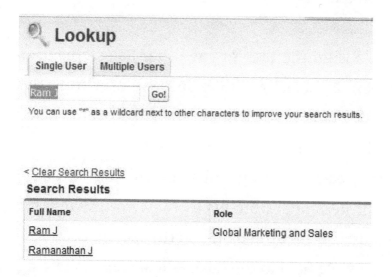

We can also search for and assign a subject for any task by clicking on the lookup icon next to the Subject field in the Task Information section. The standard subjects that are available for a task include Call, Send Letter, Send Quote and Other.

Following image displays the list of subjects that are displayed in a separate window when we click on the lookup icon next to Subject.

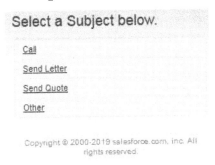

**Other task information:** We can assign the task to a lead or a contact in the Related To section of the Edit Task page.

The Related To dropdown list is activated when we select the option Contact in the Name dropdown list.

We can set a reminder for our task in the Reminder section and can also attach files in reference to the task in the Attachments section of the Task Edit page. We can set the reminder for the task on occurrence date or few days before the task.

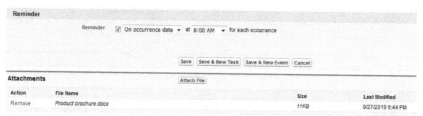

**Recurrence:** Our leads could be occupied with multiple commitments during many instances. As a result, our sales professionals may be required to follow up on a constant basis over a period of time with their leads in order to move the sales process forward.

For e.g. A lead might be attending internal company meetings over many days and hence he may not be able to allot time to the sales representative for product demonstration meeting. As a result, the sales representative will be required to follow up with the lead by calling daily, once in a week or once in a month to request for a product demonstration meeting.

Salesforce users can create a recurring series of tasks that will repeat as per a set frequency for a period ranging from the recurrence start date to recurrence end date. Users can click on the Create Recurring Series of Tasks checkbox in the Recurrence section of Task Edit page as shown in the following image.

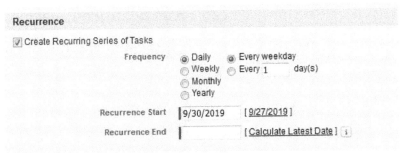

We can set the frequency for the task as daily, weekly, monthly or yearly. We can set the granular level detail for every frequency option. For e.g. We can set the specific day in a week when the task should recur when we select the Weekly frequency option. Similarly, we can set the specific day in a month such as 2$^{nd}$ Friday in a month when we select the Monthly frequency option for the recurring task.

We select the weekly frequency option and set the task to recur once every week on every Monday.

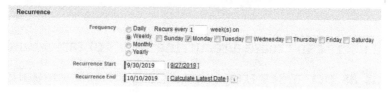

We can click on the Save button to store the task details for the lead. If we now go back to the lead detail screen, we can find the list of activities with Open Status in the Open Activities section. We can observe an icon, next to the subject item in the list, which indicates the task is a recurring one.

We can close an activity or task by clicking on the Cls link in the Action column of the activity list in the Open Activities section.

The Status field in the Task Information section of the Task Edit page is set to Completed by default.

We can click on the Save button to store the task details. Once we change the task status to Completed and save the details, the task is automatically moved from the Open Activities section to Activity History section.

**Sending Individual Email:** We can directly send emails from Salesforce to Leads from the Lead Detail page.

We can send an email to the lead by clicking on the Send an Email button in the Activity History or HTML Email Status section. Following image displays the respective sections in the Lead Detail page.

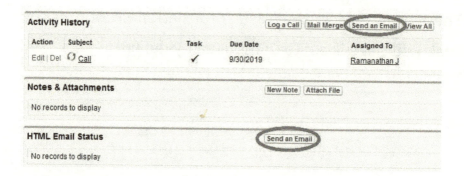

Once we click on the Send an Email button located in either of the sections in the Lead Detail page, we can view the Send an Email page from where we can send an email. Following image displays the same.

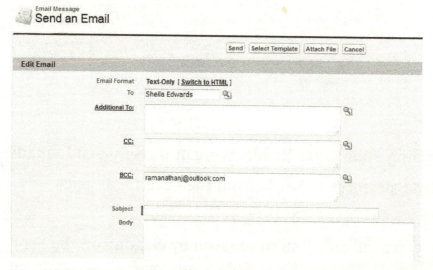

The Send an Email page is like any standard compose email page. We can select additional recipients, enter subject and compose message from this page. We can also select a pre-defined template to send an Email to recipients. We can click on the Select Template button located at the top of the Send an Email page to view the list of available Email templates.

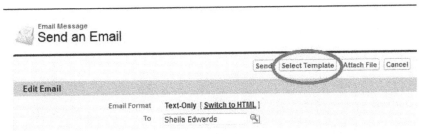

The following image shows the list of available Email templates that are visible in a new window.

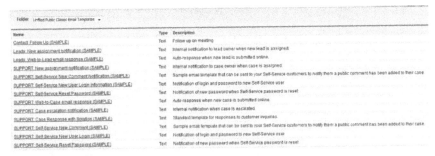

If we select the Contact: Follow Up(Sample) email template, then the email subject and message is pre-filled according to the template content.

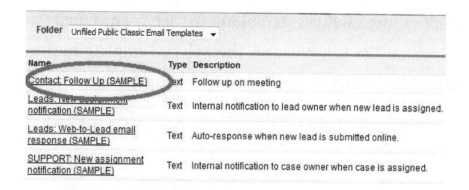

Following image displays the email message that is pre-filled according to the selected email template.

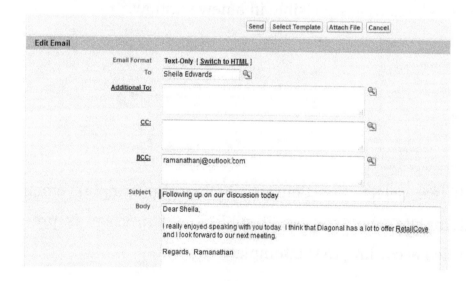

We can select the email format as Text-Only or HTML based by clicking on the Text-Only or the Switch to HTML link at the top of the Edit Email page.

We can use additional formatting options such as font type, size, text color, background color, hyperlinks and so on with HTML email format.

We can verify the message contents and then click on Send button to send the email to the recipient.

Once we send the email to a lead, this sent email will be available in the Activity History section of the Lead Detail page. The sent email will also be available in the HTML Email Status section of the Lead Detail page in case if we use the HTML email format.

Following screenshot displays the portion of the Lead Detail page with the email activity log.

| Activity History | Log a Call | Mail Merge | Send an Email | View All | | | | |
|---|---|---|---|---|---|---|---|---|
| Action | Subject | | | | Task | Due Date | Assigned To | Last Modified Date/Time |
| Edit ; Del ○ Call | | | | | ✓ | 9/30/2019 | Ramanathan J | 9/27/2019 11:24 PM |
| Edit ; Del Email, Following up on our discussion today | | | | | ✓ | 9/28/2019 | Ramanathan J | 9/28/2019 1:33 AM |

| Notes & Attachments | New Note | Attach File |
|---|---|---|
| No records to display | | |

| HTML Email Status | Send an Email | View All | | |
|---|---|---|---|---|
| Action | Subject | Date Sent | Date Opened | # Times Opened |
| Edit ; Del Email, Following up on our discussion today | | 9/28/2019 1:33 AM | | 0 |

**Mass Email Leads:** Our sales professionals may come across many leads from several organizations during various instances. For example, a sales representative may attend a trade finance exhibition and he may meet finance directors from many companies at this exhibition.

Sales representatives would then be required to send emails to multiple leads in order to follow up with them for potential business opportunities. Salesforce users can use the Mass Email Leads feature to send emails to many leads at once. Users can click on the Mass Email Leads link in the Tools section that is located on the Leads Home page to access this feature.

Following image displays the Tools section in the Leads Home page.

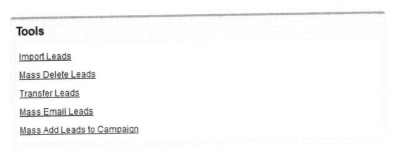

**Tools**

Import Leads

Mass Delete Leads

Transfer Leads

Mass Email Leads

Mass Add Leads to Campaign

Following steps are to be performed after we click on the Mass Email Leads link as shown above.

1. Specify the recipients who are to be included in the mass email. We can use the standard view to search for recipients or we can create a new view for this purpose. We can click on the Go button to extract lead data from the view.

Mass Email
**Recipient Selection**

Step 1. Specify the recipients to include

Select a view below that contains the recipients to be included in this email.

View:  My Leads ▾  Go!   Edit | Create New View

We can select multiple leads from the data generated after running the lead view. We can then click on the Next button located at the bottom right side of the page to proceed to the next step.

2. We can now look at the list of available email templates and select the one that meets our requirements. We can preview the email template content by clicking on the Preview link. This will open the email template preview in a new window.

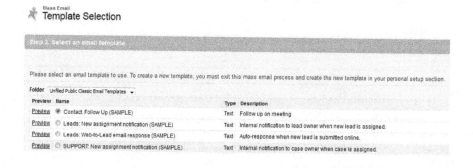

We can select an appropriate email template and click on the Next button to proceed to the next step.

3. We can set the processing and delivery options in this step. We are required to set a Mass Email name in this step.

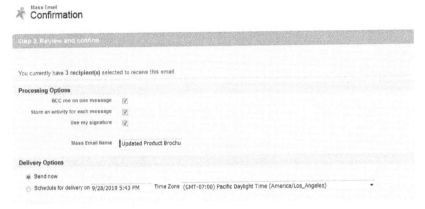

Mass Email
Confirmation

Step 3: Review and confirm

You currently have 3 recipient(s) selected to receive this email.

**Processing Options**

BCC me on one message ☑

Store an activity for each message ☑

Use my signature ☑

Mass Email Name │ Updated Product Brochu

**Delivery Options**

⦿ Send now

◯ Schedule for delivery on 9/28/2019 5:43 PM    Time Zone  (GMT-07:00) Pacific Daylight Time (America/Los_Angeles)    ▾

We can BCC our self on one message, create an activity for each message or use our signature by selecting the appropriate options in the Processing Options section as shown above.

We can set the option for either sending the mass email now or schedule the email to be sent at a specified time from the Delivery Options section.

We can click on the Send button once we have selected the appropriate processing and delivery options.

We can now observe the Mass Email Complete message in the last step of the Mass Email wizard.

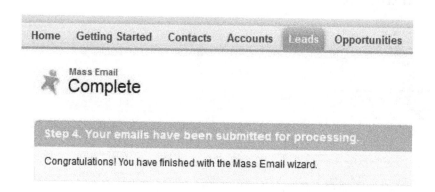

We will receive the mass email details on our email ID that we have mentioned in our Salesforce profile. We can also view the mass email details by clicking on the Mass Emails link in the Email section of My Settings page.

Following images display the mass email details within the My Settings page.

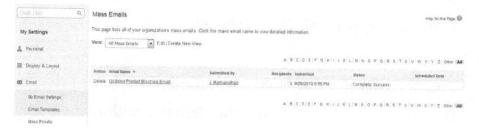

We can click on any of the links in the Mass Email column as shown in the above image to view more details about a specific email. The following image displays the mass email details.

Mass Emails
« Back to List: Mass Emails

| Mass Email Detail | | Delete |
| --- | --- | --- |
| Email Name | Updated Product Brochure Email | |
| Email Template or List Email | Contact Follow Up (SAMPLE) | |
| Scheduled Delivery | | |
| Status | Complete: Success | |
| Addressed to | 3 | |
| Sent to | 3 | |
| Store an activity for each message | ✓ | |
| BCC me on one message | ✓ | |
| Use my signature | ✓ | |
| Created By | Ramanathan J | |
| Created Date | 9/28/2019 5:55 PM | |

**Transfer Leads:** When we are working in a sales team, we may be occasionally allocated a lead that was previously owned by some other sales representative. In other instances, we may allocate a lead, who we are presently tracking, to some other Salesforce user or sales team member.

We may transfer leads within the sales team to distribute the workload. We may also want to transfer leads from a junior sales professional to a more experienced sales representative in case a specific lead has to be handled with finesse.

We can transfer leads in Salesforce by clicking on the Transfer Leads link in the Tools section within the Leads home page.

**Tools**

Import Leads

Mass Delete Leads

Transfer Leads

Mass Email Leads

Mass Add Leads to Campaign

We can transfer leads from one Salesforce user to other from the Mass Transfer Leads page. We can enter user names in the Transfer From and Transfer To fields. We can search for users in the lookup window which we can access by clicking the lookup icons that are located next to the Transfer From and Transfer To fields.

We can enter various criteria to filter leads records before transferring them from one user to other.

For example, suppose we want to transfer some of the leads from the insurance industry from one user to another. We can enter the user details in the Transfer From and Transfer To fields. We then enter criteria as Industry equals Insurance. Finally, we can click on Find button to extract lead records as per the specified criteria.

Following image displays the Mass Transfer Leads page.

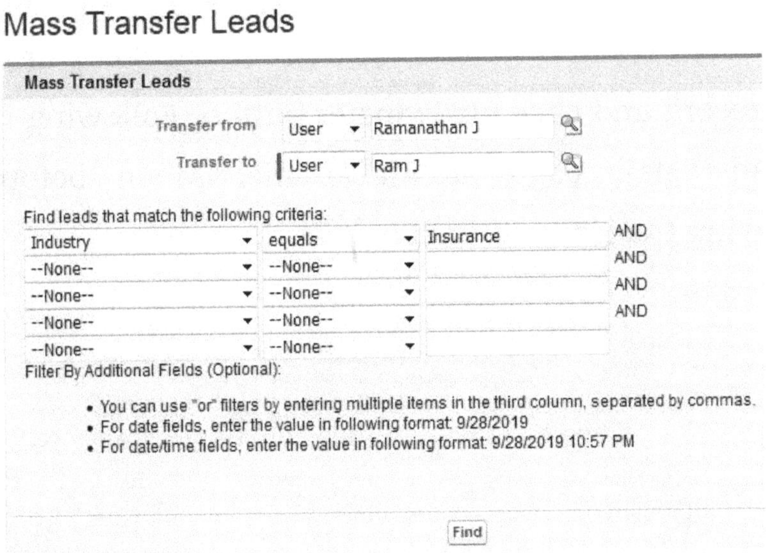

Mass Transfer Leads

Following image displays the search results as per the specified criteria.

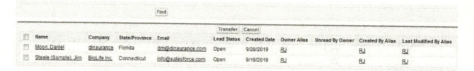

We can select leads from the search results by clicking on the checkbox next to the record. Subsequently, we can click on the Transfer button to transfer lead ownership from one user to other.

For example, suppose we want to transfer the ownership of the lead Mr. Daniel Moon whose details are displayed in the search results. We can click on the checkbox next to this record and click on Transfer button. Following is the lead detail page of Mr. Daniel Moon before transferring the lead ownership.

Following is the lead detail page of Mr. Daniel Moon after transferring the lead ownership.

Mr. Daniel Moon

Show Feed

Back to List: Mass Emails

Open Activities [0]  |  Activity History [0]  |  Notes & Attachments [0]  |  HTML Email Status [0]  |  Campaign History [0]

**Lead Detail**

Edit | Delete | Convert | Clone | Find Duplicates

| | |
|---|---|
| Name | Mr. Daniel Moon |
| Title | Director Finance |
| Email | dm@dinsurance.com |
| Phone | (786) 402-9900 |
| Lead Status | Open |

| | |
|---|---|
| Lead Owner | Ram J [Change] |
| Company | dinsurance |
| Industry | Insurance |
| No. of Employees | 1,000 |
| Lead Source | |

We can now observe that the lead owner name has changed.

We can also quickly change lead ownership by clicking on the Change link next to the Lead Owner field in the Lead Details page.

We can select a new owner for the lead in the subsequent page. We can also select the Send Notification Email checkbox if required. We can then click on the Save button to store the new lead ownership details.

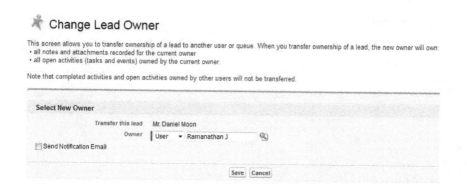

### Change Lead Owner

This screen allows you to transfer ownership of a lead to another user or queue. When you transfer ownership of a lead, the new owner will own:
• all notes and attachments recorded for the current owner
• all open activities (tasks and events) owned by the current owner

Note that completed activities and open activities owned by other users will not be transferred.

**Select New Owner**

Transfer this lead Mr. Daniel Moon

Owner | User ▾ | Ramanathan J |

☐ Send Notification Email

Save   Cancel

When we transfer the lead ownership, all notes and attachments uploaded by the current lead owner for the specified lead will be transferred to the new owner. Similarly, all open tasks or activities will be allotted to the new owner. However, completed activities or tasks will not be transferred.

**Import Leads:** We often tend to store lead details at various sources such as Email contacts, Smartphone address book and so on. However, we can consolidate lead details in Salesforce by importing the lead data from various sources.

We can click on the Import Leads link in the Tools section of Leads home page to access the Data Import Wizard.

Following image displays the Import Leads link in the Tools section within Leads home page.

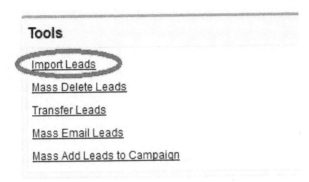

The Data Import Wizard comprises of three phases namely Choose data, Edit mapping and Start import.

**Choose Data:** We can select the type of objects i.e. Standard or Custom for import. We need sufficient permissions to import custom objects. In this case, we will select the Lead standard object.

We can specify in the subsequent step whether we want to add new records, update existing records or add new and update existing records. In this case, we select the Add new records criteria.

We can select additional criteria for adding new record. We can specify how to match lead by i.e. whether by name or email. This selection will enable Salesforce to determine whether to add new record or to update any existing record. In this case, we will select the option None because our lead data comprises of new records.

We can also assign source to the new leads. This can be useful if we have collected multiple lead records from one source such as a seminar or conference. In this case, we select the Trade Show as the option.

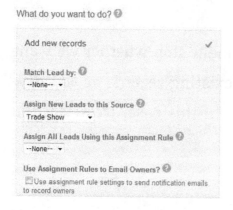

We upload the CSV file in the next step. This can be a Outlook, ACT!, Gmail, or standard CSV file.

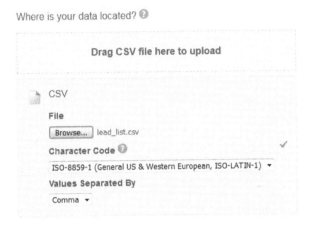

Following image displays all the steps in the Choose Data phase mentioned earlier.

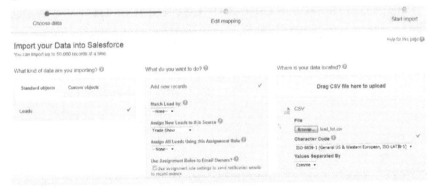

We can click on the Next button and proceed to the next step in data import process.

**Edit Mapping:** We can change the mapping between Salesforce object and CSV Header in the Edit Mapping phase if required.

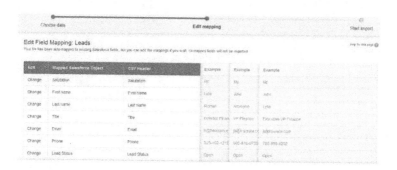

We can click on the Change link in the Edit column for any Mapped Salesforce object or CSV Header that we want to alter. Following image displays the mapping window for Salesforce objects and CSV Headers.

We can select the appropriate Salesforce field that we want to map to a CSV header and then click on the Map button.

The Data Import Wizard will highlight any CSV Header in the import data that is not yet mapped to a Salesforce field. For example, Province CSV header in our lead import data is not yet mapped to a Salesforce field.

| | | | | |
|---|---|---|---|---|
| | | | | Almost done |
| | Choose data | | Edit mapping | |
| Change | Phone | Phone | | 305-402-4212 |
| Change | Lead Status | Lead Status | | Open |
| Change | Company | Company | | finsurance |
| Change | Industry | Industry | | Insurance |
| Change | Street | Street | | 2401 Bel Meac |
| Change | City | City | | Miami |
| Map | Unmapped | Province | | Florida |

We can click on the Map link against the Unmapped CSV Header to map the same with a Salesforce field. In this case, we will select the State/Province Salesforce field to map with the Province CSV Header in our lead import data.

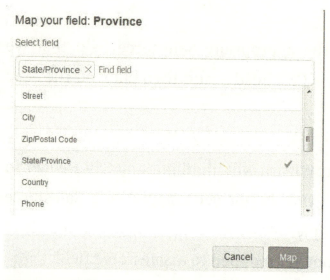

We can click on the Map button and observe that all CSV Headers in our import data are mapped to appropriate Salesforce fields.

We can then click on the Next button to proceed to the next phase of the Data Import Wizard.

**Start Import:** We can review the import information in this phase. This includes our selection criteria, mapped fields that will be included in import and the unmapped fields that will be excluded from import.

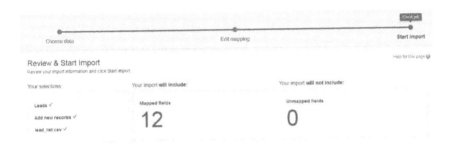

We can click on the Start Import button to start the data import process. We can view the data upload status in the Bulk Data Load Job Detail page once the import process is completed.

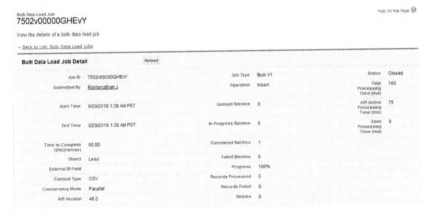

We can now go to the Leads home page and select the All Open Leads option from the View drop down list. This is because all the lead data that we imported in the previous steps have the Lead Status as Open.

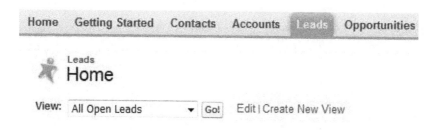

We can now observe the following list of leads that were imported earlier.

Thus, we have uploaded our lead data that is available in the form of a CSV file into Salesforce. We can upload up to 50,000 records into Salesforce at a time.

**Create new lead view:** When we are working in a big sales team, there may be many sales professionals who could be working on several leads at any moment. However, we might be interested in extracting details of certain leads. For example, we could be working on leads from a certain city or industry. In such cases, we can create a new lead view in Salesforce. This new lead view will filter and extract lead data as per our specified criteria.

We can create a new lead view in Salesforce by clicking on the Create New View link located next to the View drop down list at the top of the Leads home page.

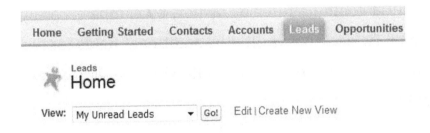

**Enter View Name:** We need to enter a view name in the subsequent page for creating new view. A view unique name is automatically generated when we enter the view name.

We will be creating a new lead view that will extract only those lead records that belong to the Aerospace and Defense industry.

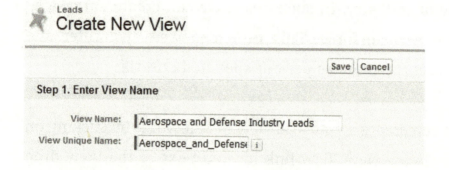

Leads
**Create New View**

| | Save | Cancel |

**Step 1. Enter View Name**

View Name:    Aerospace and Defense Industry Leads

View Unique Name:    Aerospace_and_Defense  i

**Specify Filter Criteria:** We now specify the filter criteria. The criteria could be filter by owner, by campaign or by additional fields. We will filter by additional fields for our example. We will specify the following values for our example:

1. Select Industry from the Field drop down list
2. Select Equals from the Operator drop down list
3. Enter Aerospace & Defense in the Value text box

We can use multiple additional fields for specifying filter criteria. For example, we can extract lead records for those companies from the insurance industry that are located in New York. Each of the filter criteria is joined by AND logical operator.

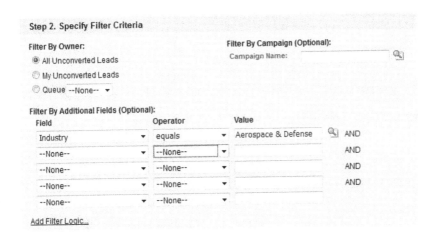

**Step 2. Specify Filter Criteria**

Filter By Owner:
- ◉ All Unconverted Leads
- ○ My Unconverted Leads
- ○ Queue --None-- ▾

Filter By Campaign (Optional):
Campaign Name: [              ] 🔍

Filter By Additional Fields (Optional):

| Field | Operator | Value | |
|-------|----------|-------|---|
| Industry ▾ | equals ▾ | Aerospace & Defense 🔍 | AND |
| --None-- ▾ | --None-- ▾ | | AND |
| --None-- ▾ | --None-- ▾ | | AND |
| --None-- ▾ | --None-- ▾ | | AND |
| --None-- ▾ | --None-- ▾ | | |

Add Filter Logic...

**Select fields to display:** We select the fields that are to be displayed in the view from a list of available fields. We can add, remove, or change the order of display for selected fields in the view by using the respective buttons.

We will select the name, company, industry, city, phone, email and lead status fields to display in our view.

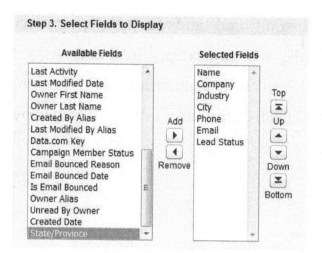

**Restrict visibility:** We can restrict the visibility of the new view by selecting either one of the following options.

We can finally create the new view by clicking on the Save button. The newly created view will be available in the Leads view drop down list.

**Creating custom lead fields:** We may often gather additional information about the leads that cannot be captured with standard Salesforce fields. We can create custom lead fields to capture additional lead related information in such cases.

For example, suppose our company sells software products for Analytics, Database and Mobile technologies. Our sales representative could come to know about the primary technology requirements for a lead during the course of various interactions.

We cannot store the value for primary technology requirement in a standard Salesforce field while creating or editing a lead. Hence, it becomes necessary to store the value for primary technology requirement in a custom lead field.

We can click on the Setup link that is located on the top right side of any Salesforce page.

We can now focus on the Build -> Customize -> Leads section in the Setup page.

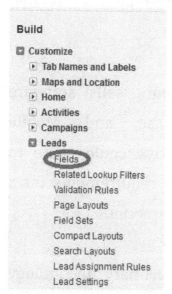

We can now click on the Fields link within Leads section. We can observe the Lead Fields page when we click on the above link. Following image describes this page.

## Lead Fields

This page allows you to specify the fields that can appear on the Lead page. You can create up to 100 Lead custom fields.

Note that deleting a custom field will delete any filters that use the custom field. It may also change the result of Assignment or Escalation Rules that rely on the custom field data.

[ Set History Tracking ]

### Lead Standard Fields
Lead Standard Fields Help ?

| Action | Field Label | Field Name | Data Type | Controlling Field | Indexed |
|---|---|---|---|---|---|
| | Address | Address | Address | | |
| Edit | Annual Revenue | AnnualRevenue | Currency(18, 0) | | |
| Edit | Campaign | Campaign | Lookup(Campaign) | | |
| Edit | Company | Company | Text(255) | | ✓ |
| Edit | Company D-U-N-S Number | CompanyDunsNumber | Text(9) | | |
| | Created By | CreatedBy | Lookup(User) | | |
| Edit | Data.com Key | Jigsaw | Text(20) | | |
| Edit | Description | Description | Long Text Area(32000) | | |
| Edit | Do Not Call | DoNotCall | Checkbox | | |
| Edit | Email | Email | Email | | ✓ |

The initial section in the Lead Fields page provides a list of standard lead fields that are available when we create a new lead. Some of the standard lead fields include lead name, company name, phone, email and so on.

The subsequent section in the Lead Fields page describes the Lead Custom Fields.

### Lead Custom Fields & Relationships

[ New ] [ Map Lead Fields ] [ Field Dependencies ]

No custom fields defined

We can click on the New button in the Lead Custom Fields & Relationships section to create new custom lead field. We can create a new custom lead fields by completing the following steps.

**Choose the field type:** We can select the data type of the custom lead field in this step.

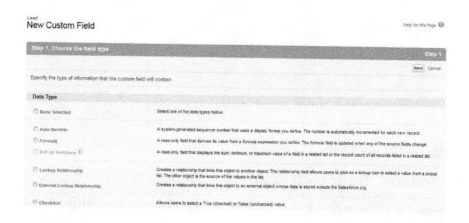

For our example, we will select the Picklist data type for the custom lead field to store the primary technology requirement value for any lead.

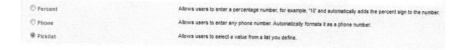

We can click on the Next button to proceed to the next step for creating a custom lead field.

**Enter the Details:** We can enter the following details in this step.

Field Label value is displayed page layouts, reports and lead views. We enter the field label value as Primary Technology Requirement for our example custom lead field.

We can enter values that will be used in a picklist by entering one value per line in the Values field. Values in the picklist can be displayed alphabetically or as per the order mentioned in the Values field. Similarly, we can use the first value as default value if required. We enter the values Analytics, Database and Mobile in the Values field for our example.

Field Name value is automatically generated when we enter the Field Label value. We can enter the description and help text in the respective fields while creating the custom lead field if required. Similarly, we can set the custom lead field to have mandatory value before saving the record by clicking on the Required check box.

The following screenshot describes the various details that are entered while creating a new custom lead field for Primary Technology Requirement.

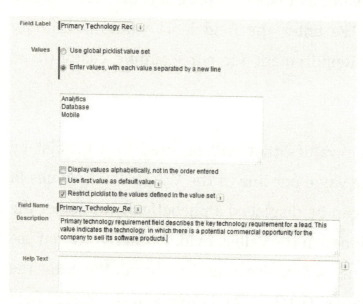

We can click on the Next button to proceed to the next step.

**Establish field-level security:** We can select the field-level security for the custom lead field according to various profiles. We can select if a field is to be made visible or is to be made read-only for available profiles.

We will select the option to make the custom lead field visible for all profiles.

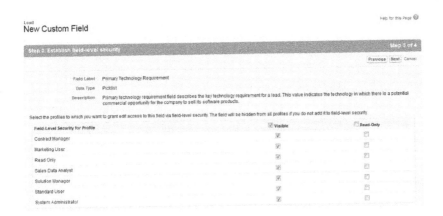

We can now click on the Next button to proceed to the next step.

**Add to page layouts:** We can select the page layouts that should include the custom lead field. This field will be added as the last field in the first two column section of these page layouts. We will select the Lead Layout as the page layout that will include our example custom lead field.

We will be required to customize the page layout in case we would like to change the location of the field on the page.

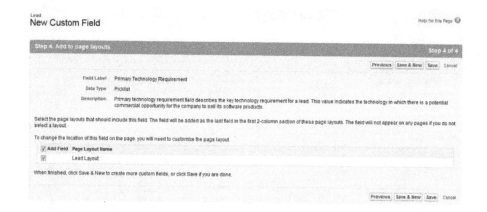

We can click on the Save button to create the new custom lead field. We can click on Save & New button if we want to create more custom fields.

We can now view the new custom lead field Primary Technology Requirement in the Lead Custom Fields & Relationships section within the Lead Fields page.

| Lead Custom Fields & Relationships | | New   Map Lead Fields   Field Dependencies | | | | | Lead Custom Fields & Relationships Help   ? |
|---|---|---|---|---|---|---|---|
| Action | Field Label | API Name | Data Type | Indexed | Controlling Field | Modified By | |
| Edit : Del : Replace | Primary Technology Requirement | Primary_Technology_Requirement__c | Picklist | | | Ramanathan J. 9/30/2019 1:10 AM | |

If we now click on the link for any lead in the Leads home page, we can view the new custom lead field that we created in the previous steps.

We can click on the Edit button to select a value for the new custom lead field.

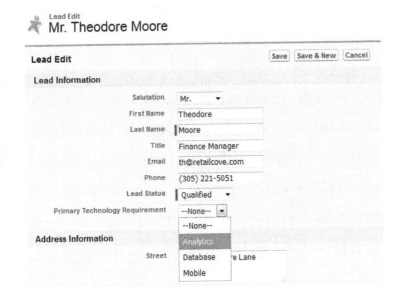

The selected value for the custom lead field will now appear in the lead detail page.

**Converting a lead:** When we interact with a lead over a period of time to identify potential opportunities for new business, we might discover that the lead has a possible need for purchasing products or services from our organization.

In such cases, we can convert the lead in Salesforce to mark the start of sales process. We can convert a lead into accounts, contacts, opportunities and tasks. We should qualify a lead before converting it. A lead cannot be viewed or edited as lead once it is converted. However, leads that are converted can be viewed in lead reports.

We can convert any lead in Salesforce by going to the lead detail page and clicking on the Convert button.

We create a new account when we convert a lead in the subsequent page. This new account will indicate the organization that the lead represents. We specify the record owner who will be handling this account. We also create a new opportunity while converting a lead. An opportunity represents the potential business with the account. We can mention the account name and briefly describe the potential business in the Opportunity field.

Converted Status value is Qualified by default because leads cannot be converted before they are qualified. We can select the checkbox next to Send email to owner field if we want to notify the record owner about the lead conversion.

We can create a new task while converting a lead. This new task could have subject values as Send letter, Call, Send Quote or Other. We can assign status, due date and priority as well as provide comments to the task. We can set a reminder for our task if required.

We can finally convert the lead by clicking on the Convert button. The following image describes the details mentioned earlier for converting a lead.

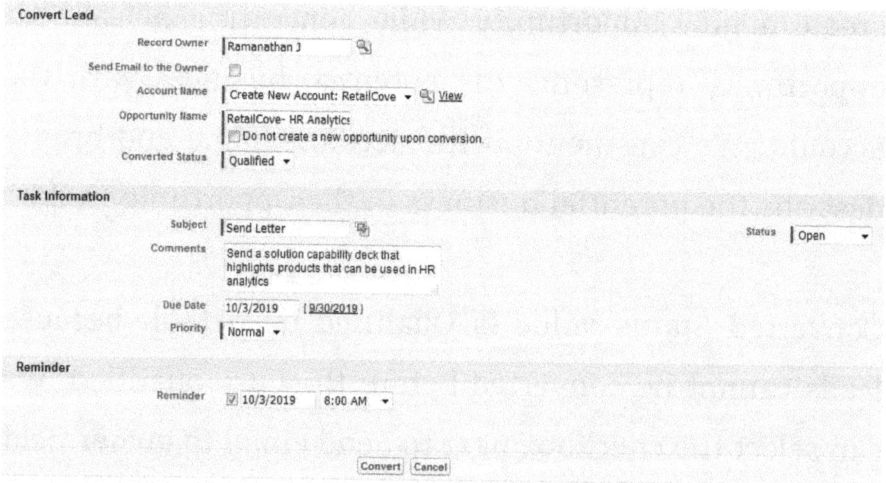

Once we convert a lead, we can observe that the organization associated with a lead is now available as an Account record in Salesforce.

We can also observe that the details of the individual that were earlier stored as a lead record is now converted into a contact which in turn is associated with an account.

A new opportunity with a default stage as Prospecting is also created when a lead is converted.

Activity history and all open activities that were earlier associated with a lead will now be linked to a contact which in turn represents an account. Activity history and all open activities will also be related to an Opportunity once a lead is converted.

| Open Activities | | | New Task  New Event | | |
| --- | --- | --- | --- | --- | --- |
| Action | Subject | Name | Related To | | |
| Edit | Cls | Call | Sheila Edwards | RetailCove- HR Analytics solution | | |
| Edit | Cls | Send Letter | Sheila Edwards | RetailCove- HR Analytics solution | | |
| Edit | Cls | Call | Sheila Edwards | RetailCove- HR Analytics solution | | |

| Activity History | | Log a Call  Mail Merge  Send an Email  View All | | |
| --- | --- | --- | --- | --- |
| Action | Subject | | Name | Related To |
| Edit | Del | Call | | Sheila Edwards | RetailCove- HR Analytics solution |
| Edit | Del | Mass Email: Follow up on meeting | | Sheila Edwards | RetailCove- HR Analytics solution |
| Edit | Del | Email: Following up on our discussion today | | Sheila Edwards | RetailCove- HR Analytics solution |

Similarly, all notes and attachments that were earlier associated with a lead will be linked to an account once this lead is converted.

| Notes & Attachments | | | New Note  Attach File  View All | | | | Notes |
| --- | --- | --- | --- | --- | --- | --- | --- |
| Action | Type | Title | | Related To | Last Modified | | Created By |
| Edit | View | Del | Attachment | Product brochure.docx | | Call | 9/27/2019 6:52 PM | | Ramanathan J |

Lead conversion is an important milestone in the overall sales process. Salesforce users can track business opportunities and overall customer relationship in a holistic manner through Accounts, Contacts, Opportunities and Activities once a lead is converted.

# ACCOUNTS

An account can be any organization that our company does business with. An account can be an existing customer, prospect, partner or a competitor.

The primary objective of a Customer Relationship Management (CRM) solution such as Salesforce is to provide a centralized platform for its users to manage account related information and interactions. You can handle all account related data and activities from the Accounts application in Salesforce.

Salesforce users can obtain a strategic view for all the companies that they are interacting with from the Accounts application in Salesforce. Leads are non-relational and hence we may not be able to establish organizational relationship between multiple persons when these individual details are stored as leads. However, we can track organizational hierarchy and multiple individuals within the same company when we store the company detail as Account and individuals working in the company as Contacts.

Accounts application in Salesforce provides a single point of reference to monitor contacts, activity history, open tasks, opportunities and associated documents.

**Creating new account:** We can access Accounts application in Salesforce by clicking on Accounts link that is located in the horizontal tab menu at the top of any Salesforce page.

We can create a new account by clicking on the New button within the Recent Accounts section that is located on the Accounts home page. Recent Accounts section displays a list of accounts that were recently created, modified or viewed. We can view the list of recent accounts as per the required criteria by selecting the appropriate option from the drop down list that is located on the right side within the Recent Accounts section.

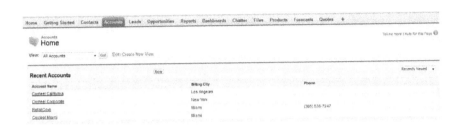

Following page is displayed when we click on the New button within the Recent Accounts section.

As we can observe in the above image, Account Name is the minimum information that we are required to enter when we create a new account in Salesforce. We can also store additional details such as account type, industry, description and so on while creating a new account if required.

**Example for a new account:** We will consider the following case for creating a new account in Salesforce. Suppose our company sells software products in database, analytics and mobile technologies. We sold a database software product to a customer called SteelSource few years back.

SteelSource manufactures and sells steel plates. SteelSource has a corporate office in New York and manufacturing plants at Los Angeles and Miami locations.

SteelSource has expanded its business significantly and has generated a lot of profits since we last sold the database product to them. Our sales team has decided to target this company to create new business for our analytics and mobile technology products.

Hence, we now want to store the details of this existing customer into Salesforce as a new account. This will enable our sales team to keep a track of all interactions with the customer from a single platform.

We will enter the details to create a new account for SteelSource Corporate as shown in the following image.

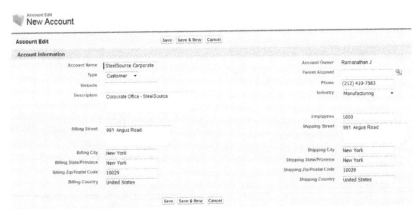

We can click on the Save button to create a new account. We can click on the Save & New button if we want to save the current details and proceed to create a new account.

We can observe the details of the newly created account in the Account Details page. The Account Details page will also contain details regarding contacts, opportunities, activities, attachments and cases related to the account.

We can similarly create two new accounts for the two manufacturing plants of SteelSource that are located at Miami and Los Angeles locations.

The following image displays the account detail page for SteelSource Miami account.

The following screenshot describes the account detail page for SteelSource Los Angeles account.

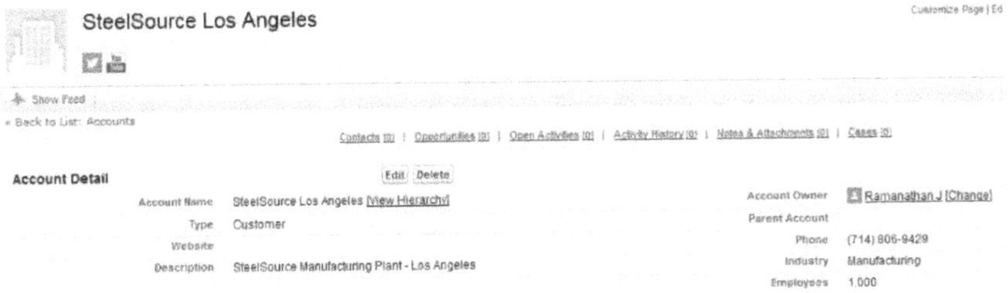

SteelSource Los Angeles

Customize Page | Ed

Show Feed
« Back to List: Accounts

Contacts [0] | Opportunities [0] | Open Activities [0] | Activity History [0] | Notes & Attachments [0] | Cases [0]

**Account Detail**                        Edit   Delete

| | | | |
|---|---|---|---|
| Account Name | SteelSource Los Angeles [View Hierarchy] | Account Owner | Ramanathan J [Change] |
| Type | Customer | Parent Account | |
| Website | | Phone | (714) 806-9429 |
| Description | SteelSource Manufacturing Plant - Los Angeles | Industry | Manufacturing |
| | | Employees | 1,000 |

In this way, we have created three accounts in Salesforce for SteelSource Corporate, Miami and Los Angeles entities. However, SteelSource Miami and SteelSource Los Angeles are subsidiaries of SteelSource Corporate. We can depict this hierarchical structure between various corporate entities by creating an account hierarchy in Salesforce.

**Creating new account hierarchy:** We can create a hierarchy between various accounts by specifying the parent account value in the account detail page.

We will now specify SteelSource Corporate as the parent account for SteelSource Miami account. We can go to the account detail page for SteelSource Miami and click on the Edit button to enter the value in the parent account field.

We can click on the lookup icon next to the Parent Account field to search for accounts.

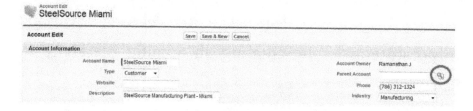

We can select the SteelSource Corporate value from the Lookup list as the parent account for our example. We can now click on the Save button to store the parent account detail for our account. The following screenshot describes the parent account value for SteelSource Miami in the account detail page.

We can similarly provide parent account value for SteelSource Los Angeles as SteelSource Corporate. The following image describes the parent account value for SteelSource Los Angeles in the account detail page.

If we now click on the View Hierarchy link that is located next to the Account Name field in the Account Detail page, we can observe the hierarchy between various accounts.

The following screenshot describes the hierarchy between SteelSource Corporate, Miami and Los Angeles accounts.

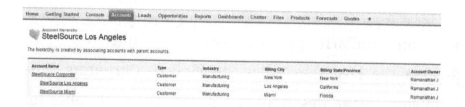

**Merge Accounts:** Companies or accounts often transform in many ways over a period of time. Some companies merge together or one could acquire the other organization. An organization could also shut down one location and concentrate operations and employees at one location for achieving better efficiency.

Salesforce users can use the Merge Accounts functionality to combine different accounts by clicking on the Merge Accounts link in the Tools section within the Accounts home page.

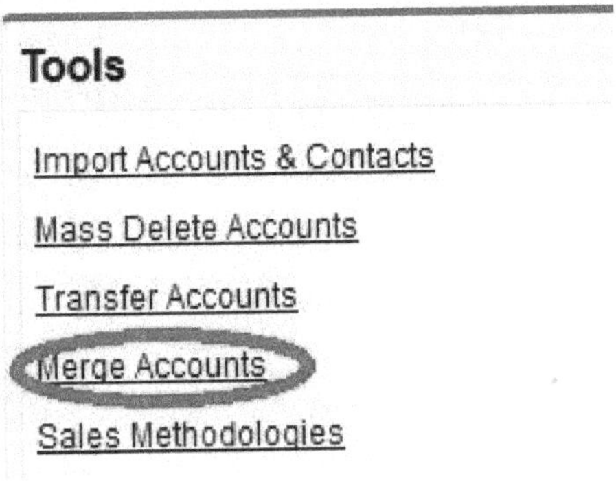

**Tools**

Import Accounts & Contacts

Mass Delete Accounts

Transfer Accounts

Merge Accounts

Sales Methodologies

For our example, let us assume that SteelSource Corporate is shifting its Corporate office from New York to Miami. We will use the merge accounts functionality to update this detail.

**Select records to merge:** We can select up to three records to merge into one in the first step. We can enter a key word and click on the Find Accounts button to search for the accounts that we wish to merge. We will select the accounts SteelSource Corporate and SteelSource Miami for our example.

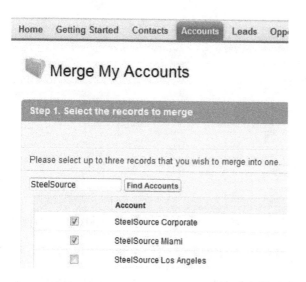

We can click on the Next button now to proceed to the next step.

**Select the values to retain:** We will now select the values that are to be retained once the account records are merged. Fields that contain conflicting data are highlighted. All activities and attachments will be associated with the merged record.

Since SteelSource Corporate will now be shifted to the Miami location, we will retain SteelSource Miami as the Account Name. We will use the phone, billing and shipping address of Miami location in the merged record. However, we will use the description as Corporate Office-SteelSource for the merged record.

The following screenshot describes the values that are to be retained.

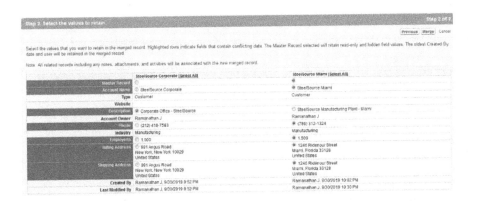

We can now click on the Merge button to merge the two accounts. If we now go to the Account Details page for SteelSource Miami, we can observe that the Description field for this account contains the value Corporate Office-SteelSource which was the description value provided for SteelSource Corporate account.

All other values in the merged record are retained as per the options selected in the previous step.

Following screenshot highlights the Account Detail page for SteelSource Miami account after merging the accounts.

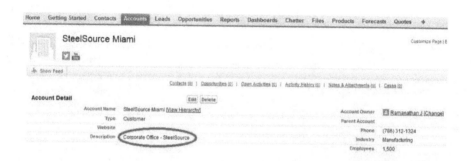

The account hierarchy that was created before accounts were merged is no longer valid. We can view this by going to the account detail page for SteelSource Los Angeles and clicking on the View Hierarchy link.

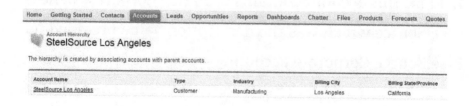

We can observe that the hierarchy between SteelSource Corporate and SteelSource Los Angeles which existed before account merger is now automatically removed. We can follow the steps as described earlier to create a new account hierarchy between SteelSource Miami and SteelSource Los Angeles.

The following screenshot describes the updated account hierarchy.

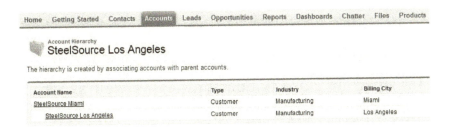

**Transfer Accounts:** As we saw in case of leads, we might be required to transfer accounts between various Salesforce users. We can transfer accounts among users for various reasons such as to distribute workload among different users or to hand over big accounts to senior sales professionals.

We can transfer accounts by clicking on the Transfer Accounts link in the Tools section of Accounts Home page.

**Tools**

Import Accounts & Contacts

Mass Delete Accounts

Transfer Accounts

Merge Accounts

Sales Methodologies

We can provide the user details in the Transfer from and Transfer to fields. We can also choose if we want to transfer open or closed opportunities as well as cases from the existing account owner to the new account owner by selecting the respective check boxes.

We can find accounts by providing various criteria. We can provide multiple conditions to filter account records. These conditions are joined by AND logical operator.

New account owner will also gain ownership of any notes, contacts, opportunities or open activities that belongs to the current account owner once the account records are transferred.

Following screenshot describes the Mass Transfer Accounts page.

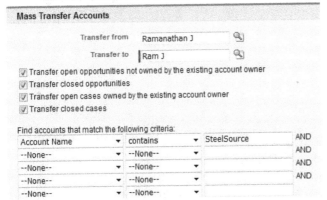

## Mass Transfer Accounts

This screen allows you to transfer an account from one user to another. When you transfer o transferred account:

- Any notes that belong to the existing owner.
- All contacts that belong to the existing owner.
- All opportunities (including closed opportunities if you select the Transfer closed
- All open activities assigned to the existing owner. Note that completed activities w
- The new owner might need to edit sharing.

**Mass Transfer Accounts**

| Transfer from | Ramanathan J |
| Transfer to | Ram J |

☑ Transfer open opportunities not owned by the existing account owner
☑ Transfer closed opportunities
☑ Transfer open cases owned by the existing account owner
☑ Transfer closed cases

Find accounts that match the following criteria:

| Account Name | ▾ | contains | ▾ | SteelSource | AND |
| --None-- | ▾ | --None-- | ▾ | | AND |
| --None-- | ▾ | --None-- | ▾ | | AND |
| --None-- | ▾ | --None-- | ▾ | | AND |
| --None-- | ▾ | --None-- | ▾ | | |

We can search for accounts as per the specified criteria. We can select the appropriate account from the search results by clicking on the check box next to the account record. We can then click on the Transfer button to transfer the account to the new user.

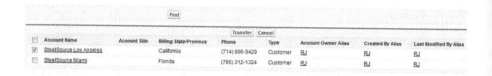

We can go to the Account Details page once we have transferred the ownership to view the new owner details.

**Import Accounts and Contacts:** We can import accounts and contact data by following a process that is similar to the one that we performed while importing lead data. We can click on the Import Accounts & Contacts link within the Tools section in the Accounts home page to import accounts and contacts data using the data import wizard.

## Tools

**Import Accounts & Contacts**

Mass Delete Accounts

Transfer Accounts

Merge Accounts

Sales Methodologies

The data import wizard allows users to import accounts and contacts data by choosing data and by editing the mapping between the Salesforce fields and CSV headers.

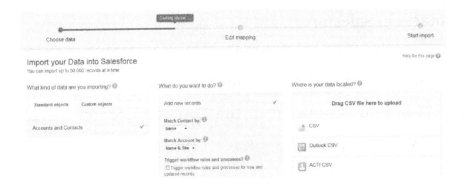

All CSV headers in the data that are mapped to Salesforce fields will be imported.

**Creating Contacts for Accounts:** When we do business with a customer, we are going to interact with individuals who work for the customer organization in various roles. We can store details of these individuals who are working for a customer or an account by creating Contacts in Salesforce.

Contacts are associated with accounts in Salesforce. We can also understand reporting structure or chain of command among various individuals within an account by defining reporting relationships between various contacts in Salesforce.

We can create a new contact for an account by clicking on the New Contact button in the Contacts section within Account Detail page.

We can also create a new contact from the Contacts page that can be accessed by clicking on the Contacts tab in the horizontal tab menu.

We will now create a new contact that we have created for SteelSource Miami account. Last Name and Account Name are mandatory fields that are to be filled while creating a new contact for an account. Address details for a contact are automatically extracted from the account address information. We can enter details for other optional fields such as Reports to, Department, Email or Phone if required. The following image describes the page for creating a new contact.

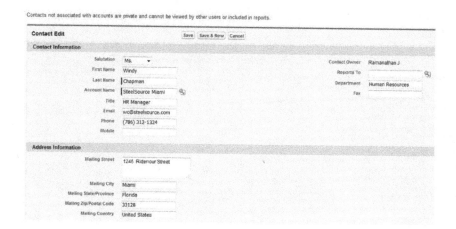

We can click on the Save button to store the details of the new contact for an account.

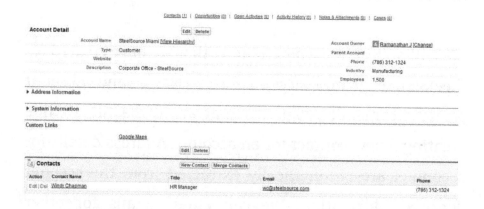

The contact detail is now available in the Account Detail page.

**Opportunities:** We can track potential business deals by creating opportunities in Salesforce. We can create new opportunity by clicking on New Opportunity button in the Opportunities section within the Account Detail page.

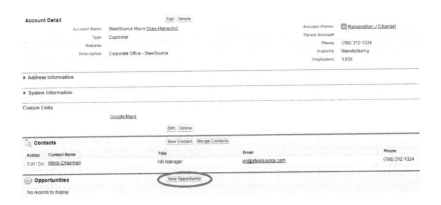

We can enter details for the new opportunity that we are presently tracking in the following page.

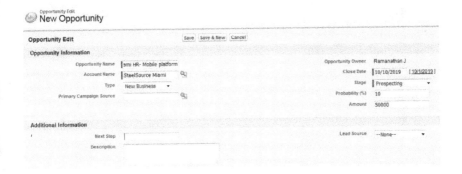

We are required to mention the opportunity name, account name, close date and stage values while creating a new opportunity. We can click on the Save button to store the new opportunity details.

The new opportunity record is now available in the Account Detail page.

| Opportunities | | | | New Opportunity | | | |
| --- | --- | --- | --- | --- | --- | --- | --- |
| Action | Opportunity Name | | | | Stage | Amount | Close Date |
| Edit \| Del | SteelSource Miami HR- Mobile platform | | | | Prospecting | $50,000.00 | 10/10/2019 |

**Open Activities:** We can create a new task or a new event from the Account Detail page for any account. A new task can include calling a contact, sending a letter and so on.

We can create a new task or a new event by clicking on the respective buttons in the Open Activities section within the Account Detail page.

| Open Activities | New Task | New Event |
| --- | --- | --- |
| No records to display | | |

Following image describes the task edit page.

We need to assign a subject, task owner, task status and priority while creating a new task. We can set a due date and reminder for the task. We can allocate this task to a contact and account.

As we observed in case of leads, we can set this task to be a recurring one in case we have to repeat this task regularly over a period of time such as weekly or monthly. We can also upload attachments such as proposal documents or presentation deck to a task if required.

We can click on the Save button to create the new task. The new task record is now available in the Open Activities section within the Account Detail page.

Following image describes the task detail located within the Open Activities section.

| Open Activities | | | New Task | New Event | | | | | | Open |
|---|---|---|---|---|---|---|---|---|---|---|
| Action | Subject | Name | Related To | | Task | Due Date | Status | Priority | Assigned To | |
| Edit \| Cls | Call | Windy Chapman | SteelSource Miami | | ✓ | 10/3/2019 | Open | Normal | Ramanathan J | |

We can change the Task Status to Completed and click on Save once we have performed the task. The task is moved to the Activity History section when the Task Status is converted to Completed.

| Activity History | | | Log a Call | Mail Merge | Send an Email | View All | | | |
|---|---|---|---|---|---|---|---|---|---|
| Action | Subject | Name | Related To | | Task | Due Date | Assigned To | Last Modified Date/Time | |
| Edit \| Del | Call | Windy Chapman | SteelSource Miami | | ✓ | 10/3/2019 | Ramanathan J | 10/1/2019 6.34 PM | |

As we saw in case of leads, we can also send an email to various individuals or contacts by clicking on the Send an Email button within the Activity History section of the Account Detail page. We can assign an Email template or choose between text only or HTML formatted email if required. Activity records represent the series of interactions between sales professionals and various stakeholders from an account and are thus key to ensure an effective customer relationship management.

# PRODUCTS AND PRICE BOOKS

Products represent products and services that a company sells to its customers. Sales professionals associate products to multiple opportunities that they may pursue while engaging various accounts. Products associated with certain prices is the core component of a sales professional's value proposition when he is trying to secure a new business for an account.

Salesforce users can access Products home page by clicking on the Products tab in the horizontal tab menu.

**Creating new products:** We can create new products in Salesforce by clicking on the New button in the Recent Products section that is located within the Products home page.

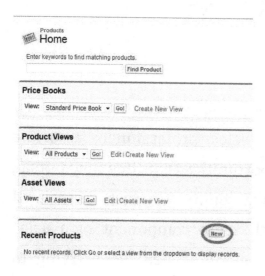

Following image describes the subsequent page for creating new product:

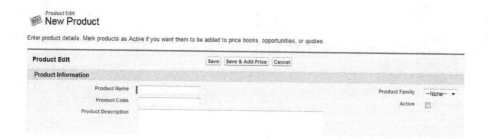

We are required to provide Product name while entering product details. We can provide a unique identifier for product code if required. We can also enter a product description and assign the product to a product family as per our requirements. We need to mark the product as Active if we want to add the product to price books, opportunities or quotes.

We will now create products for our example organization. As we saw earlier, our company sells software products in database, analytics and mobile technologies. Hence, we will create three new products in Salesforce by entering the necessary details.

Following screenshot describes the product details for the database product sold by our example organization.

We can click on Save button to store the product details or we can click on the Save & Add Price button to store the product detail and to immediately enter the standard price for the product as well.

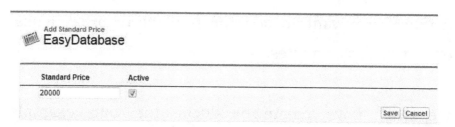

We will enter the standard price of USD 20000 for our EasyDatabase product. We can click on Save button to store the standard price details for our product.

Following screenshot describes the product detail page.

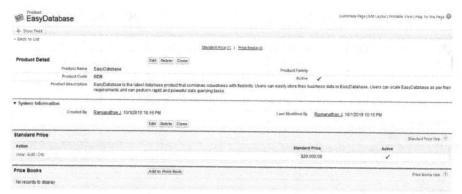

We will create two more products and their respective standard prices for our example organization by following the steps mentioned earlier.

Following image highlights the Recent Products section within the Products home page. The Recent Products section lists the three products sold by our example organization.

---

**Recent Products**

New

| Product Name | Product Code | Product Description |
|---|---|---|
| EasyMobile | EMB | EasyMobile is an intuitive and simple reporting dashboard app for your smartphones. Y |
| EasyAnalytics | EAL | EasyAnalytics is the latest software solution that uses powerful Artificial Intelligence tec |
| EasyDatabase | EDB | EasyDatabase is the latest database product that combines robustness with flexibility. I requirements and can perform rapid and powerful data querying tasks. |

---

**Product Search:** We can search for products by entering relevant keywords in the product search text box next to the Find Product button. The product search text box is located at the top of the Products home page.

Products
**Home**

Enter keywords to find matching products.

Find Product

The following product search result page will be displayed if we enter the keyword database in the product search text box.

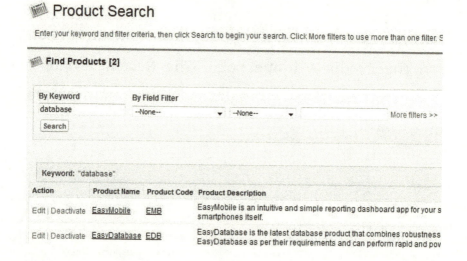

We can directly go to the product details page by clicking on any link in the Product Name column within the search results as shown above.

We can also search for products by providing field filter criteria. We can use product details related fields such as product name, code or description to filter our search results. We can also enter multiple field filter related conditions to further narrow down our search results.

**Creating new price books:** We can create and maintain price books by clicking on the Manage Price Books link in the Maintenance section within Products home page.

We can create new price book by clicking on the New button in the Recent Price Books section within the Price Books page.

We can enter price book name and description in the price book edit page. We can set the price book as Active by selecting the checkbox next to it. We can also create a new price book by cloning an existing price book such as Standard Price Book if required.

We will create a new standard price book for the EasyDatabase product that our example organization sells. We will select the checkbox for Active option.

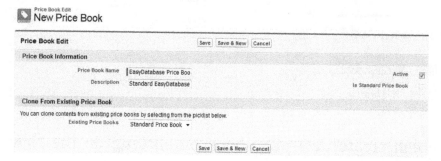

We can click on the Save button to store the new price book details. We can now view the price book details as shown in the following screenshot.

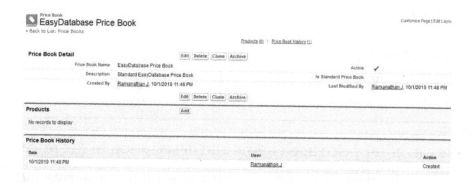

We can add products to the price book by clicking on the Add button within the Products section of the Price Book details page.

We can click on the checkbox next to the product that we want to include in a price book. For our example, we will select the checkbox next to the EasyDatabase product and click on the Select button to include the product in the price book that we created in the previous steps.

Product Selection for
**Price Book EasyDatabase Price Book**

Enter your keyword and filter criteria, then click Search to begin your search. Click More filters to use more than one filter. Search results include all records that match both your keyword and filter entries.

Select | Cancel

**Find Products**

By Keyword | By Field Filter
| --None-- | --None-- | More filters >>

Search

A B C D E F G H I J K L M N O P Q R S T

| Product Name ↑ | Product Code | Standard Price | Product Description | Product Family |
|---|---|---|---|---|
| EasyAnalytics | EAL | $40,000.00 | EasyAnalytics is the latest software solut... | |
| EasyDatabase | EDB | $20,000.00 | EasyDatabase is the latest database prod... | |
| EasyMobile | EMB | $50,000.00 | EasyMobile is an intuitive and simple repo... | |

We can enter the list price in the subsequent page if required. List prices are custom prices that can be used to offer products at different prices to various subsets of customers such as different market segments or regions. We can create custom price books to store the list prices for our products.

We will enter the list price as USD 15000 for the EasyDatabase product and click on Save button to store the details.

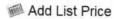 Add List Price

You need to specify a List Price if you want to add a product to the price book.

| Product | Price Book | Use Standard Price | List Price | Active |
|---|---|---|---|---|
| EasyDatabase | EasyDatabase Price Book | $20,000.00 ☐ | 15000 | ☑ |

Save   Save & More   Cancel

We can now view the product along with list price in the Products section within the Price Book Detail page.

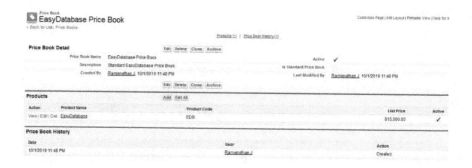

**Custom price books:** We can create custom price books to store different list prices for our products. We can use custom price books to offer our products at different prices to various customer segments.

For example, we can offer our products at discounted rates to not for profit organizations as compared to other companies. We can create one custom price book with product list price for not for profit organizations and another custom price book with a different product list price for other companies.

We will create two custom price books for our example organization. One custom price book will be used to store product list prices for domestic customers and the other price book will contain the product list prices for international customers.

We will perform the steps that were described earlier to create two custom price books.

Following screenshot describes the page for domestic price book detail:

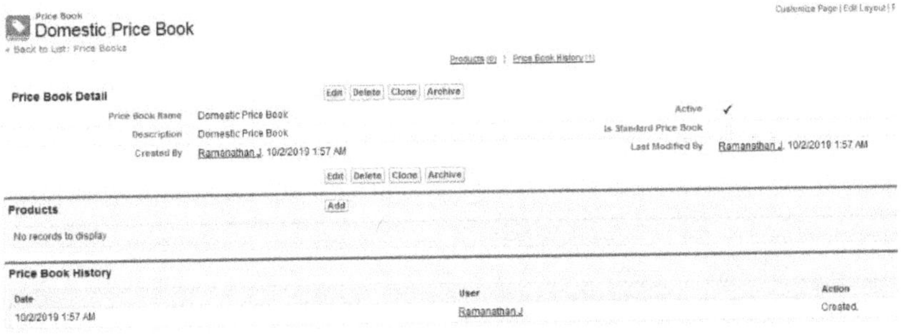

Following image describes the page for international price book detail:

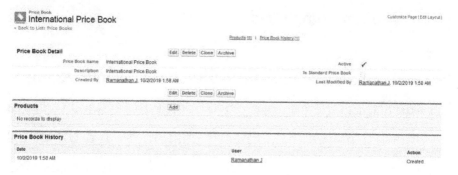

We will add the products sold by our example organization to the domestic price book. We will click on the Add button in the Products section of Price Book Detail page and then click on the relevant products that are to be included in the price book.

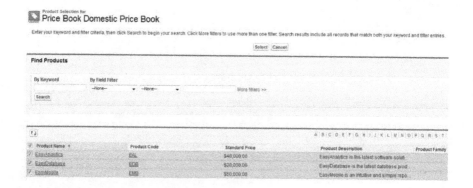

We can now enter the list prices for each product that is included in the domestic price book. The list price for each of the products in the domestic price book will have a discount of 10% from the standard price. This domestic price book will be applicable for domestic customers.

## Add List Price

You need to specify a List Price if you want to add a product to the price book

| Product | Price Book | Use Standard Price | List Price | Active |
|---|---|---|---|---|
| EasyAnalytics | Domestic Price Book | $40,000.00 | 36000 | ☑ |
| EasyDatabase | Domestic Price Book | $20,000.00 | 18000 | ☑ |
| EasyMobile | Domestic Price Book | $50,000.00 | 45000 | ☑ |

Save   Save & More   Cancel

We can click on Save button to store the list price for each product in the domestic price book. The following image describes the detail page for domestic price book.

We can similarly create an international price book for our products. We will provide list price at 20% discount of standard price for international customers.

We can click on Save button to store the list price details of each product in the international price book. The following image describes the international price book detail page with the list price for each product.

Our sales professionals can now assign the custom price books and products to various opportunities that they will pursue while trying to secure new business from various accounts.

# CONTACTS AND OPPORTUNITIES

Contacts are individuals from an organization with whom we do business. Unlike leads, contacts are always linked to an account. As a result, we can keep a track of interactions with various individuals in an account through contacts. We can also reporting structure between various individuals in an account by storing their details in contacts.

We earlier created a new contact for the account SteelSource Miami by clicking on the New Contact button within the Contacts section of the Account Detail page. We can also create new contacts for an account from the Contacts home page that can be accessed by clicking on the Contacts tab on the horizontal tab menu.

**Creating new contacts:** We can create new contacts for an account by clicking on the New button in the Recent Contacts section within the Contacts home page.

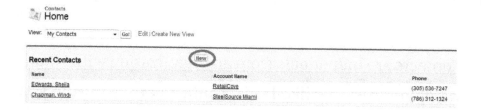

Let us consider the example account named SteelSource Miami that we created previously. Suppose our sales professional has attended a trade conference recently. He has met four individuals from SteelSource Miami at this conference.

Two of these individuals work in the Finance department while the other two persons are from the HR function. Our sales professional believes that there could be a potential chance to create new business by selling analytics or mobile software products to both departments within SteelSource Miami. We will hence create the four new contacts for SteelSource Miami account in order to track the interactions with these contacts.

Following screenshot describes the page for creating a new contact.

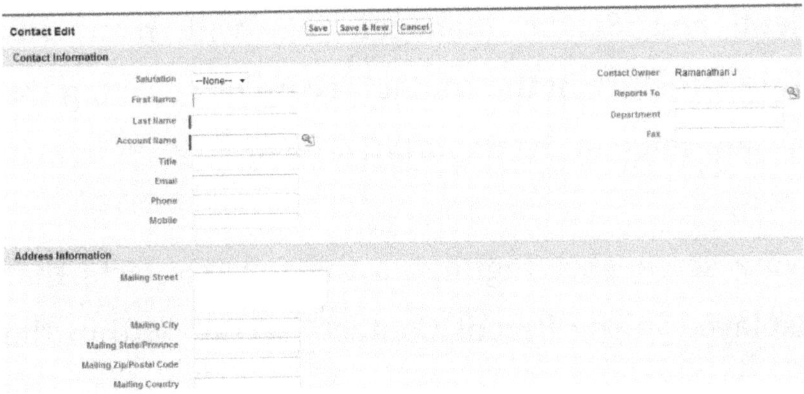

We are required to enter information for Last Name and Account Name fields while creating a new contact. We can also enter additional details for a contact such as department, address and phone if required. We can map the reporting structure between multiple contacts by entering a value in the Reports To field.

We will create the records for four contacts as specified in the earlier example. Fields in the Address Information section within Contact Edit page are automatically filled with Account address details when we select a value for the Account Name field.

Each pair of individuals from SteelSource Miami's Finance and HR departments have a designation of Vice President and Senior Manager. We will map this reporting structure in the contact record by selecting the appropriate value in the Reports To field.

Following screenshot highlights the four contacts that are displayed in the Recent Contacts section within the Contacts home page.

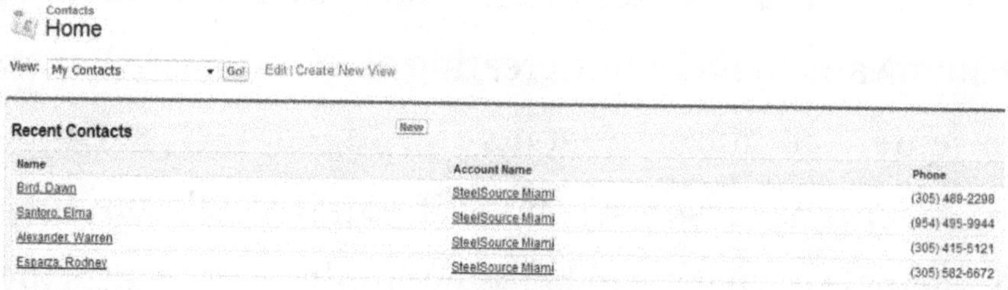

We can now click on the link for any contact to view the Contact Detail page. We can add opportunities, activities, cases or notes to a contact from the Contact Detail page.

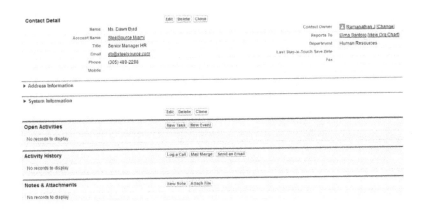

We can view the reporting structure between various contacts by clicking on the View Org Chart link next to the Reports To field in Contact Detail page.

Following screenshot describes the reporting structure between the contacts within the HR department of SteelSource Miami.

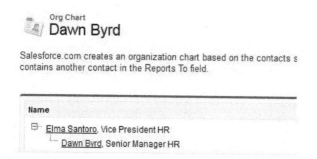

**Opportunities:** Opportunities are business deals that are currently in progress. We can create opportunities in Salesforce to track the progress of ongoing business deals with an account.

We can create an opportunity when we convert a qualified lead. We can create an opportunity for an Account from the Account Detail page. Finally, we can create an opportunity from the Opportunities home page that can be accessed by clicking on the Opportunities link in the horizontal tab menu.

**Creating new opportunity:** We will create a new opportunity from the Opportunities Home Page. We will consider our earlier example in which our sales professional believes that our company can sell its analytics and mobile software products to both Finance and HR departments of SteelSource Miami. We will create new opportunities in Salesforce to store the details of these potential business deals.

We can click on the New button in the Recent Opportunities section within Opportunities home page to create a new opportunity.

Opportunity Name, Account Name, Close Date and Stage are mandatory fields for creating a new opportunity.

Stage field values indicate the current status of the opportunity. Some of the standard values for the Stage field include Prospecting, Qualification, Needs Analysis and so on.

For example, our sales team might be compiling a value proposition for one business opportunity while another business deal might have advanced to the negotiation stage. Hence, we can edit the value for the Stage field to update the current status of an opportunity.

Every value in the Stage field has a corresponding probability value which indicates the likelihood of winning the deal. The Probability(%) field value is automatically filled when we select a value for Stage.

However, we can also enter our own value in the Probability(%) field if we have a better estimate of winning probability for an opportunity at any given stage.

We will now create an opportunity in Salesforce that will represent the new business opportunity to sell Analytics software product to the SteelSource Miami Finance department. We will assign the stage field value as Value Proposition for the opportunity. We will use the default probability value of 50%. We will select the Type field value as New Business.

Following image describes the Opportunity Edit page.

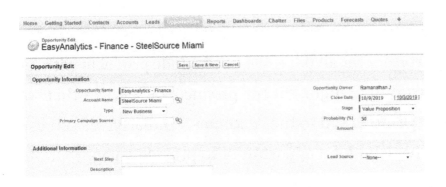

We can click on the Save button to store the new opportunity details. The Opportunity Detail page will describe the various details such as activities or notes for an opportunity.

We will create other new opportunities in Salesforce as per our example requirements. Following screenshot describes the Recent Opportunities section which includes the four opportunities that we have created so far.

| Recent Opportunities | New | |
|---|---|---|
| **Opportunity Name** | | **Account Name** |
| EasyAnalytics - HR - SteelSource Miami | | SteelSource Miami |
| EasyMobile - HR - SteelSource Miami | | SteelSource Miami |
| EasyMobile - Finance - SteelSource Miami | | SteelSource Miami |
| EasyAnalytics - Finance - SteelSource Miami | | SteelSource Miami |

**Assigning price books and products:** We can assign price books and products to opportunities from the Opportunity Detail page. We can include products with an opportunity to highlight the products or services that we are offering to sell to the customer. Similarly, we can use price book with an opportunity to provide an appropriate list price for the product.

We can assign a price book to an opportunity by clicking on the Choose Price Book button in the Products section of the Opportunity Detail page.

**Products**

Add Product | Choose Price Book | Sort

No records to display

We will select the Domestic Price Book for our example opportunity and will save the details.

Choose Price Book for
**EasyAnalytics - Finance - SteelSource Miami**

Select a price book for this opportunity. You can add products only from a single price book.

**Choose Price Book for: EasyAnalytics - Finance - SteelSource Miami**

Price Book    Domestic Price Book    ▼

Save | Cancel

We can now add product to our opportunity by clicking on the Add Product button in the Products section of the Opportunity Detail page.

**Products (Domestic Price Book)**

Add Product | Choose Price Book | Sort

No records to display

We will click on the checkbox next to the product that we want to include in our opportunity details. We will select the checkbox next to the product EasyAnalytics for our example and click on the Select button to add this product to our opportunity.

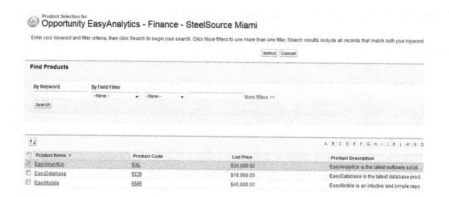

We can assign values for Quantity and Sales Price fields in the subsequent page. Sales Price indicates additional discount offered on products over the list price.

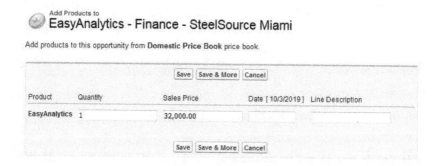

We can save the product detail for the opportunity. We can now observe the sales price and list price for the product in the opportunity detail page.

**Contact Roles:** A contact could play various roles in an account when we are trying to pursue an opportunity. For example, a contact could be an executive sponsor, decision maker or an influencer within an account. Hence, a contact could have enough leverage over the entire negotiation process. Certain contacts could determine whether we eventually win the business opportunity with an account.

We can create contact roles within opportunity detail page to capture the roles played by various contacts within an account.

We can click on the New button within the Contact Roles section of the Opportunity Detail page.

We can select various contacts and assign them the appropriate roles in the subsequent page.

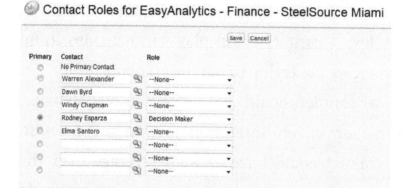

Contact Roles for EasyAnalytics - Finance - SteelSource Miami

We can click on Save to assign the contact role to the opportunity records.

**Quotes:** We can use quotes within an opportunity detail to store details of the exact price and discount that we are offering on our products to the customers.

Quotes will consider the price book and products that we selected while creating the opportunity record. We can assign product quantity and sales price in percentage while creating a new quote for an opportunity.

We can create a new quote by clicking on the New Quote button in the Quotes section within the Opportunity Detail page.

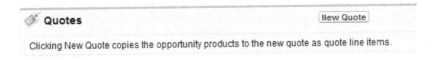

Quote name is the only mandatory field required for creating a new quote. However, we can also include additional information such as quote status, tax, shipping and handling value and description if required.

Following image highlights a portion of the Quote Edit page.

The quote will be allocated to the opportunity record upon saving.

We can view the Quote Detail page when we click on the Quote Name link in the Quotes section of the Opportunity Detail page.

We can also view the Quote Detail page by clicking on the Quotes tab in the horizontal tab menu and then clicking on a link for quote in the Recent Quotes section of the Quotes Home page.

The Quote Detail page includes quote line items as shown in the following image.

We can add new quote line item by clicking on Add Line Item button in the Quote Line Items section. We can also edit the current quote line item by clicking on the Edit link next to the respective line item.

We can enter the discount value in percentage for a quote line item in the subsequent page. We can also include sales price, quantity and line item description if required.

EasyAnalytics for Initial quote - EasyAnalytics Finance

| Quote Line Item Edit | Save | Cancel |
|---|---|---|

**Quote Line Item Information**

| Line Item Number | 00000002 | | Subtotal | $32,000.00 |
|---|---|---|---|---|
| Product | EasyAnalytics | | Discount | 5 |
| Quote Name | Initial quote - EasyAnalytics Finance | | Total Price | $32,000.00 |
| List Price | $36,000.00 | | Line Item Description | estimate with 5% discou |
| Sales Price | 32,000.00 | | | |
| Quantity | 1.00 | | | |

Following screenshot displays the quote line item with the updated total price after entering the discount percentage value.

| Quote Line Items (Domestic Price Book) | | Add Line Item | Edit All | Sort | | | | Quote Line Items (Domestic Price Book) Help |
|---|---|---|---|---|---|---|---|---|
| **Action** | **Product** | **Sales Price** | **Quantity** | | **Subtotal** | **Discount** | **Total Price** | **List Price** |
| Edit / Del | EasyAnalytics | $32,000.00 | 1.00 | | $32,000.00 | 5.00% | $30,400.00 | $36,000.00 |

Thus, we can use quote line items to store various combinations of sales price, discount and quantity values for an opportunity.

# MARKETING APP

# CAMPAIGNS

Companies allocate marketing budgets to execute marketing activities in any target market. Companies intend to build brand awareness about their products or services in a market by running various types of marketing activities in a market.

We can track various types of marketing activities by using the Campaigns application within the Marketing App of Salesforce.

A campaign is any marketing activity that we intend to administer or track in Salesforce. Some of the common types of campaigns or marketing activities include tradeshows, seminars, webinars, email marketing, print advertising, public relations outreach and social media engagement.

We can access the Campaigns application by clicking on the Campaigns tab in the horizontal tab menu for the Marketing App.

**Creating new campaigns:** We can create a new campaign by clicking on the New button in the Recent Campaigns section within the Campaigns home page.

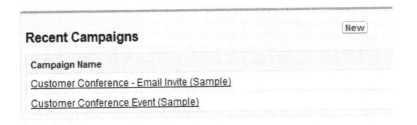

Campaign Name is a mandatory field when we create a new campaign. Status field value indicates the current stage of a campaign. Status field value includes the standard values of In Progress, Planned, Completed and Aborted. We can assign a start and end date for a campaign. We can also choose campaign type value by selecting an appropriate option from the Type drop down list. Some of the values in Type drop down list includes Conference, Email, Webinar and PR.

We can provide values for budgeted cost, actual cost as well as the expected revenue fields if we intend to track these metrics for a campaign. Similarly, we can enter a percentage value for Expected Response field if we are aware of the average response rate for any type of campaign. We can use the Expected Response field value to track campaign effectiveness.

We will now create a direct email campaign in Salesforce for our example company. This email campaign will be completed in one day. We will select the checkbox for Active field and will assign the Status field value as Planned.

We can edit the campaign record later and edit the value for the Status field. This field value can be updated whenever the campaign proceeds to the next stages such as In Progress or Completed.

Following screenshot describes the Campaign Edit page that is used for creating a new campaign record.

We can click on the Save button to store the campaign record. The following image describes a portion of the campaign detail page.

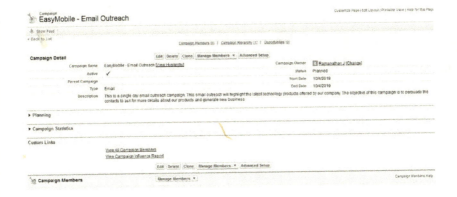

**Campaign Hierarchy:** Marketing teams often create integrated campaigns that can include multiple marketing activities. These integrated marketing campaigns provide a multi-pronged approach for building brand awareness in a target market.

For example, we can create an integrated marketing campaign to target the insurance industry for obtaining new business. We can create two components namely email outreach and conference that can be included in this integrated campaign.

We can map campaign hierarchy in Salesforce by providing a value for the Parent Campaign field while creating a new campaign or editing an existing one.

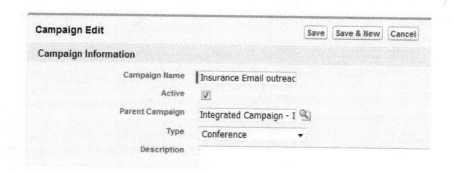

We can view the campaign hierarchy across various parent and sibling campaigns in the Campaign Hierarchy section within the Campaign Detail page.

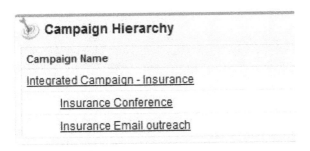

Campaign Hierarchy

Campaign Name

Integrated Campaign - Insurance

    Insurance Conference

    Insurance Email outreach

**Adding members to campaign:** We execute a marketing campaign to build brand awareness among a target audience. This target audience can include leads or contacts from various accounts.

We can add members to a campaign by clicking on the Manage Members menu in the Campaign Members section within Campaign Detail page.

We can search for members and add them to a campaign or we can import a file that contains member data. Similarly, we can search for campaign members and edit their details or we can import a file with updated member data.

We will search for members and them to our campaign by clicking on the Add Members-Search link within the Manage Members menu as shown in the above image. Our email outreach campaign will target contacts that belong to the accounts from the Manufacturing industry.

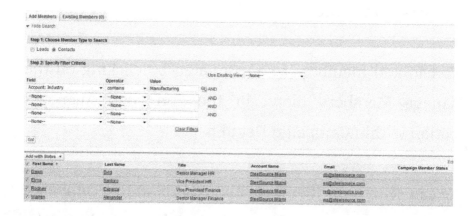

We select the member type in the initial step. A member can be a lead or a contact. We select the option Contacts for our example. We can specify the filter criteria in the subsequent step. We specify the filter criteria as industry value containing manufacturing term for our example. We can click on Go button to generate a list of contacts or leads.

We can select the contacts or leads that we want to include in the campaign by clicking on the appropriate check box. Subsequently, we can click on the Add with Status menu and select either Sent or Responded option to add the contacts as campaign members. We will select the Sent option for our example.

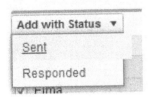

The contacts are now included as members in a campaign. Current members in a campaign can be viewed in the Existing Members tab within the Manage Members page.

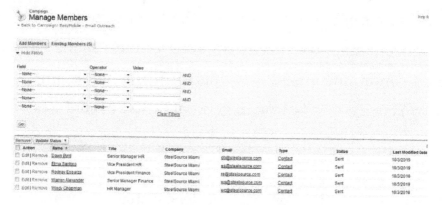

We can change the status for any campaign member by clicking on Edit link next to the respective record.

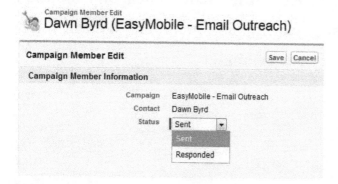

We can click on Save to update the status value for a campaign member.

The list of status values will change depending upon the Campaign type. For e.g. campaign with type value as

Email will have status values as Sent or Responded. However, campaign with type value as Conference will have status values as Invited, Registered, Attended or No Show.

**Adding opportunities to campaign:** When we execute a marketing campaign, we can expect positive responses from some of the campaign members. Sales representatives can subsequently interact with these campaign members to discover opportunities for new business. In these cases, a campaign becomes instrumental for creating new business opportunities.

We can create new opportunity for a campaign by clicking on the New Opportunity button in the Opportunities section within the Campaign Detail page.

**Campaign Hierarchy**

Campaign Name

EasyMobile - Email Outreach

**Opportunities**                                    New Opportunity

No records to display

We can create a new opportunity by following the steps as described earlier.

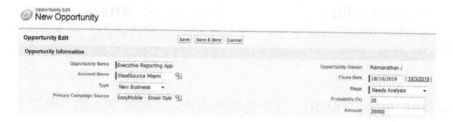

We can click on Save to store the opportunity details for a campaign. The campaign for which we created the opportunity is now visible in the Campaign Influence section of the Opportunity Detail page.

**Campaign Reports:** Campaigns application include standard reports such as Campaign ROI Analysis Report, Campaign Member Analysis Report and Campaign Revenue Report. We can access the campaign standard reports from the Reports section in the Campaigns Home Page.

## Reports

Campaign ROI Analysis Report

Campaign Member Analysis Report

Campaign Revenue Report

The Campaign ROI Analysis Report describes key metrics such as campaign type, campaign status, responses, won opportunities, value of won opportunities and so on.

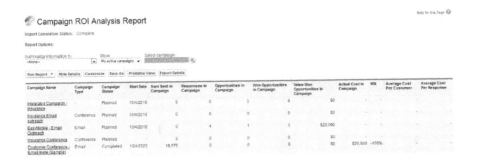

We can summarize the report by various criteria such as Campaign Status, Campaign Type or Owner.

The Campaign Member Analysis Report describes the member status for various campaign types. We can use this report to understand the member engagement for multiple campaigns.

## Campaign Member Analysis Report

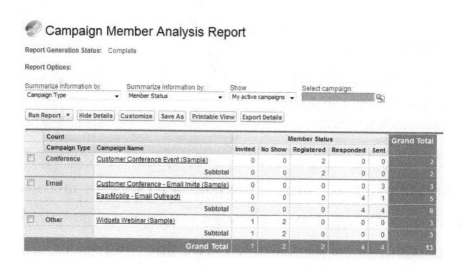

Report Generation Status: Complete

Report Options:

| Summarize information by: | Summarize information by: | Show | Select campaign: |
|---|---|---|---|
| Campaign Type | Member Status | My active campaigns | |

Run Report ▼ | Hide Details | Customize | Save As | Printable View | Export Details

| Count | | Member Status | | | | | Grand Total |
|---|---|---|---|---|---|---|---|
| Campaign Type | Campaign Name | Invited | No Show | Registered | Responded | Sent | |
| ☐ Conference | Customer Conference Event (Sample) | 0 | 0 | 2 | 0 | 0 | 2 |
| | Subtotal | 0 | 0 | 2 | 0 | 0 | 2 |
| ☐ Email | Customer Conference - Email Invite (Sample) | 0 | 0 | 0 | 0 | 3 | 3 |
| | EasyMobile - Email Outreach | 0 | 0 | 0 | 4 | 1 | 5 |
| | Subtotal | 0 | 0 | 0 | 4 | 4 | 8 |
| ☐ Other | Widgets Webinar (Sample) | 1 | 2 | 0 | 0 | 0 | 3 |
| | Subtotal | 1 | 2 | 0 | 0 | 0 | 3 |
| | Grand Total | 1 | 2 | 2 | 4 | 4 | 13 |

The Campaign Revenue Report displays the total revenue earned after winning a business from an opportunity which is in turn linked to a campaign.

## Campaign Revenue Report

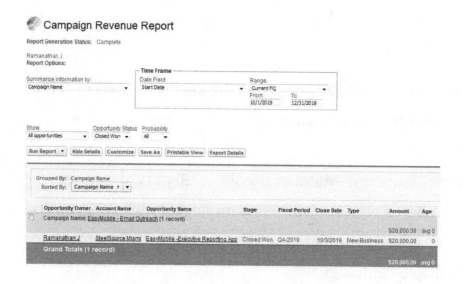

Report Generation Status: Complete

Ramanathan J
Report Options:

| Summarize information by: | | Time Frame | | |
|---|---|---|---|---|
| Campaign Name | | Date Field | Range | |
| | | Start Date | Current FQ | |
| | | | From 10/1/2019 | To 12/31/2019 |

| Show | Opportunity Status | Probability |
|---|---|---|
| All opportunities | Closed Won | All |

Run Report ▼ | Hide Details | Customize | Save As | Printable View | Export Details

Grouped By: Campaign Name
Sorted By: Campaign Name ↑ ▼

| Opportunity Owner | Account Name | Opportunity Name | Stage | Fiscal Period | Close Date | Type | Amount | Age |
|---|---|---|---|---|---|---|---|---|
| Campaign Name: EasyMobile - Email Outreach (1 record) | | | | | | | | |
| | | | | | | | $20,000.00 | avg 0 |
| Ramanathan J | SteelSource Miami | EasyMobile -Executive Reporting App | Closed Won | Q4-2019 | 10/3/2019 | New Business | $20,000.00 | 0 |
| Grand Totals (1 record) | | | | | | | | |
| | | | | | | | $20,000.00 | avg 0 |

178

# SERVICE APP

# CASES AND SOLUTIONS

We mark an important milestone in the overall customer relationship management process when we acquire new business from a customer after selling a product or service.

However, customer relationship management is an ongoing process that extends after completing a sale to an account. Customers may face issues or may require assistance when they use our company's product or service.

As a result, customers would contact our company team for after sales support or service. It is important for our company to address customer queries or support requests in a timely and effective manner. Timely post-sales support is essential to improve customer satisfaction levels and also to obtain repeat business from the existing customers in the future.

Service App in Salesforce provides a relevant platform for users to track customer support issues and solutions.

**Cases:** A case can be any request or query that originates from a customer while using a product or service. A customer can contact the company over the phone, email or contact form on the website in order to request support for resolving an issue or a query.

We can access Cases home page by clicking on the Cases tab in the horizontal tab menu within the Service App.

**Create new cases:** We can create new cases by clicking on the New button in the Recent Cases section within the Cases home page. We can also create new case for a contact or an account by clicking on the New Case button in the Cases section of Contact Detail or Account Detail page.

Following screenshot describes the Cases home page.

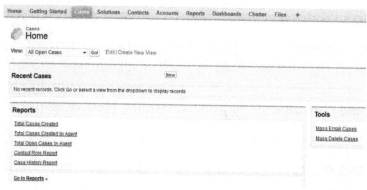

Following image describes the Case Edit page.

**Case Information:** We can enter the contact and account name for the case in the Case Information section of the Case Edit page.

**Additional Information**: We are required to select values for Status and Case Origin fields in the Additional Information section. A case can have status values of New, On Hold or Escalated. Case Origin field value indicates where the customer support request originated from i.e. Phone, Email or Web.

We can assign a priority to case in order to quickly resolve the important cases. We can also classify a case as question, problem or new feature request by selecting an appropriate value for the Type Field. We can select a value for Case Reason field to further describe the case.

**Description Information:** We can assign subject, description and internal comments for a case by entering the values for the respective fields in the Description Information section within the Case Edit page.

We can click on Save to store the case details. The following image describes the Case Detail page.

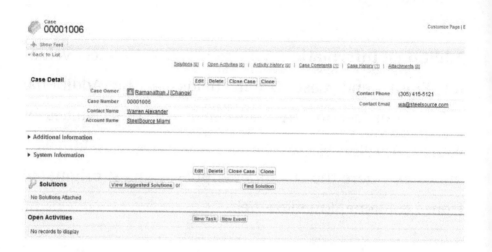

As we saw in case of leads, contacts, accounts and opportunities, we can create new activities such as tasks for a case from the Case Detail page. We can create new activities for a case in order to keep a track of all interactions that we have with a customer while addressing a query or issue.

**Closing a case:** We can close any case after we have addressed the customer issue by clicking on the Close Case button in the Case Detail page.

We are required to select the Status field value for a case as Closed in the Close Case page. We are also required to select a value for the Case Reason field. We can also provide internal comments, solution title and solution details in the Close Case page if required. We can also submit the solution information to the list of public solutions if required.

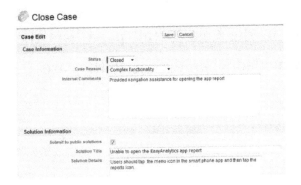

We can click on Save to close the case. We can find the log of all the updates made to a case in the Case History section of the Case Detail page.

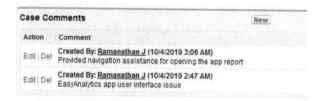

Case History

| Date | User | Action |
|------|------|--------|
| 10/4/2019 3:06 AM | Ramanathan J | Changed Case Reason from Instructions not clear to Complex functionality. Changed Status from New to Closed. Closed. |
| 10/4/2019 2:47 AM | Ramanathan J | Created. |

Similarly, we can observe all the comments that we have noted for a case so far in the Case Comments section of the Case Detail page.

Case Comments     New

| Action | Comment |
|--------|---------|
| Edit \| Del | Created By: Ramanathan J (10/4/2019 3:06 AM) Provided navigation assistance for opening the app report |
| Edit \| Del | Created By: Ramanathan J (10/4/2019 2:47 AM) EasyAnalytics app user interface issue |

The Solutions section in the Case Detail page lists the solutions that were provided when we closed the case.

Solutions    View Suggested Solutions or    Find Solution

| Action | Solution Title | Solution Number | Status | Author Alias |
|--------|---------------|-----------------|--------|--------------|
| Del | Unable to open the EasyAnalytics app report | 00000002 | Draft | RJ |
| Del | Unable to open the EasyAnalytics app report | 00000001 | Draft | RJ |

**Solutions:** We can access the Solutions home page by clicking on the Solutions tab in the horizontal tab menu for Service App.

Following image describes the Solutions home page.

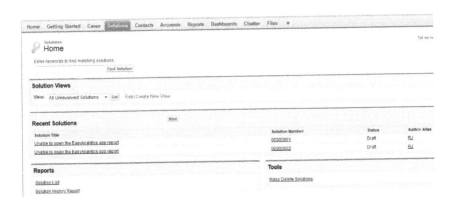

Solutions application in Salesforce acts as a knowledge repository for the customer support teams. Whenever a customer creates a new case, Salesforce users can refer to the list of solutions in order to find an approach that can resolve the case.

**Creating new solutions:** We can create a new solution by clicking on the New button in the Recent Solutions section within the Solutions home page. As we saw earlier, we can also create new solution when we close a case.

The Solution Edit page comprises of Solution Title and Solution Details fields. We are required to enter a value for Solution Title field.

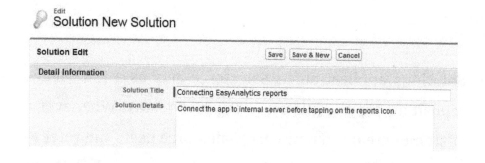

We can click on Save to store the solution details.

The following image displays the solution details page.

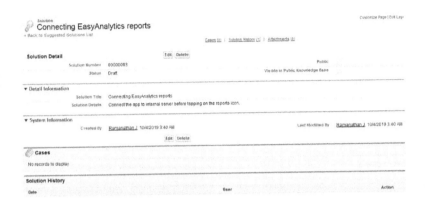

We can view the Solution Edit page when we click on the Edit button in the Solution Detail page.

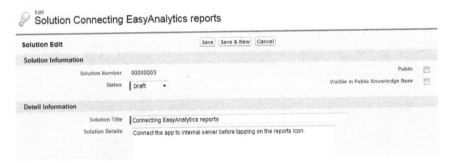

We can assign a status value for solution in the Solution Edit page. The status value can be Draft, Reviewed or Duplicate. We can also choose if we want the solution to be stored in public knowledge base or if we want the solution to be public.

**Assign solution to case:** We can assign a solution to the case by clicking on the Find Solution button in the Solutions section of the Case Detail page.

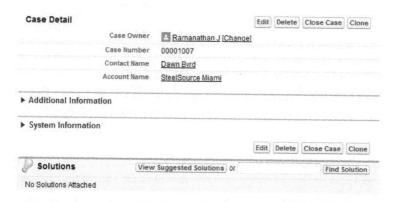

We can enter a keyword to search for solutions in the subsequent page. Subsequently, we can choose a solution from the search results and assign this solution to a case by clicking on the Select link next to the solution record.

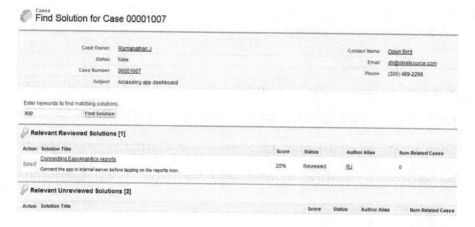

We can now view the solution record in the Solutions section of the Case Detail page.

**Solutions Reports:** We can access the reports related to solutions from the Reports section that is located within the Solutions home page.

**Solution List:** The solution list report describes the list of solutions that are currently available in Salesforce. Solution title, solution details, number of related cases and solution status are some of the key fields that are displayed in this report.

We can summarize the information in the Solution List Report by various attributes such as Status, Reviewed, Public and so on. This will group the solutions according to the value chosen for the attribute.

We can select a value in the Summarize information by drop down list to summarize solutions in the report. We can then click on the Run Report button to generate the report.

Report Options:

Summarize information by:

Status ▼

Following image describes the report that is generated when we summarize the information in the report by Status.

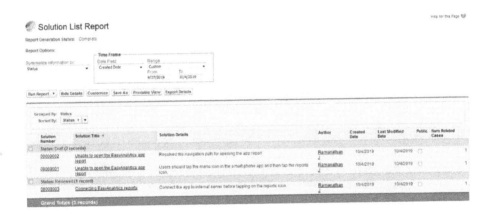

**Solution History Report:** The solution history report describes the various changes or updates that have been made to the Status field for a solution.

We can access the solution history report from the Reports section on the Solutions home page. Following image describes the Solution History Report.

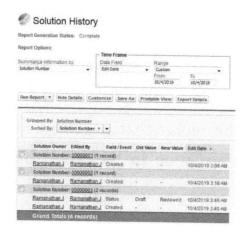

As we saw in case of the Solution List report, we can summarize information in Solution History report by various solution fields or history data. Following image describes the Solution History report when we summarize information by Status field.

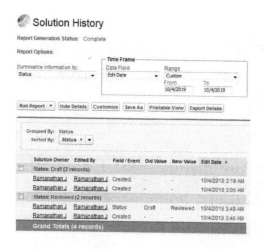

# REPORTS

Users rely on reports to obtain key insights about several metrics related to customer relationship management. Users can apply the ideas that are revealed from various reports to design effective sales and marketing strategies.

Salesforce provides various types of standard reports that can be used to obtain information about various components of customer relationship management such as leads, contacts, accounts and opportunities.

The home page for any Salesforce application such as leads or accounts contain a separate section called Reports. This Reports section lists certain key reports for users. Users can also click on the Go to Reports link within the Reports section to go to the dedicated Reports Application.

Following screenshot describes the Reports section within the Leads home page.

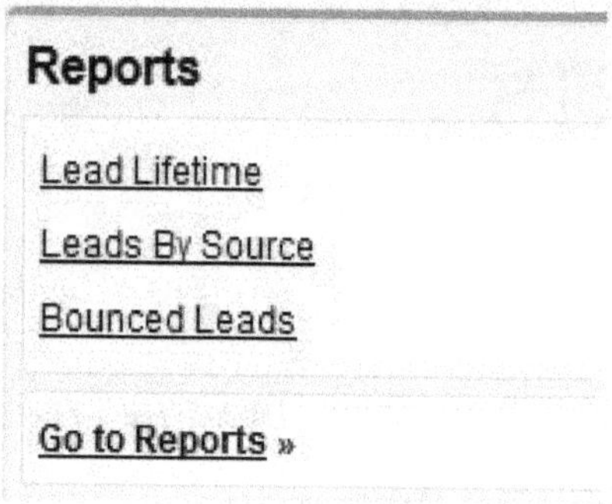

**Reports**

Lead Lifetime

Leads By Source

Bounced Leads

Go to Reports »

Similarly, the following image describes the Reports section within the Accounts home page.

**Reports**

Active Accounts

Accounts with last activity > 30 days

Account Owners

Contact Role Report

Account History Report

Partner Accounts

Go to Reports »

**Reports Application:** Salesforce users can access the Reports application by clicking on the Reports tab in the horizontal tab menu.

The following screenshot describes the Reports Application home page.

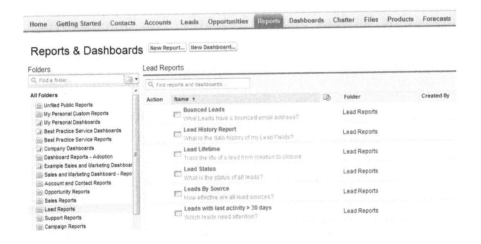

The Reports application home page comprises of two panes. The left pane of the home page lists all folders. The right pane of the home page lists all reports or dashboards that are present within a folder. Users can also create new folders to store their custom reports.

**Creating custom reports:** Sales and marketing professionals may often would like to view certain unique combination of metrics that may not be available with the standard reports. In such cases, Salesforce users can create custom reports as per their unique requirements.

Let us assume that we want to view a report that will describe the lead status across lead source and industry. We just want to view the First Name, Last Name, Title, Company/ Account Name, Industry, No. of employees, Lead Source, Email, Phone and Lead Owner for the leads in this report. We will create a new custom report to view the lead related fields as per our requirement. We will name this custom report as Custom lead status across source.

We can create a new custom report by clicking on the New Report button that is located at the top of Reports home page.

The subsequent page for creating new report comprises of two panes. We can select the Report Type from the left pane and view the report preview on the right pane. We will select the Report Type as Leads for our custom report.

We can click on the Create button to proceed to the next step for creating a new report. The subsequent page for creating a new report comprises of three sections.

**Fields:** The Fields section in the page for creating new report comprises of all the fields related to the Report Type that we selected in the previous type.

**Filters:** The Filters pane in the new report creation page includes standard filters with which we can filter the data that is to be displayed in our custom report. We can click on the Add button next to the Filters field and then enter the filter condition in the new filter row to apply custom filters for our reports.

**Preview:** The Preview pane in the new report creation page provides a preview for the report that we want to create. Users can drag and drop fields from the Fields pane on to the Preview pane to include the particular attributes in the custom report. Similarly, users can also remove columns that they do not want to be displayed in the custom report by clicking on the context menu for a column and selecting the Remove Column option.

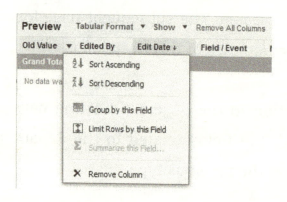

Users can click on Remove All Columns link within the Preview pane if they want to create a custom report from scratch. Users can choose if they want the custom report to be displayed in tabular, summary or matrix format. Users can also choose if they want the details to be displayed in the custom report.

We will drag and drop the fields, that we highlighted earlier, from the Fields pane on to the Preview pane to create a custom report. We will also add a filter to our custom report in order to include records for only those leads whose total number of employees is greater than 100. The following image describes the steps for creating the custom report.

We can click on the Save button to save the custom report.

We are required to specify a report name when we try to save the custom report. The report unique name field is automatically filled when we enter a report name. We can also provide a report description and a report folder location for the custom report if required.

We can click on Save to store our custom report in the specified report folder. We can now observe the custom report with updated report name in the subsequent page.

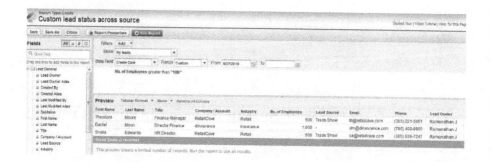

The Preview pane in the report will display a limited number of records. We can click on the Run Report button to view all the results.

Following screenshot displays the report results page.

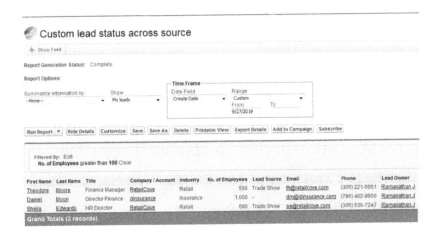

We can run a report immediately or we can set a schedule for running the reports on a daily, weekly or monthly frequency. We are required to assign a start and end date when we set a report schedule.

# CONCLUSION

Salesforce is a robust platform that can optimize the sales and marketing processes in any organization. Sales teams can utilize Sales App in Salesforce to effectively manage the leads, contacts, accounts and opportunities for their companies.

Similarly, marketing teams can plan various types of marketing campaigns from the Marketing App in Salesforce. Marketing professionals can allocate budgets to campaigns and can track the responses and opportunities that a campaign receives from the members.

Customer support teams can manage after-sales support issues or cases from the Service App in Salesforce. Support teams can create new cases and update the case status when they work towards resolving the issue. Support teams can create a knowledge repository by creating and storing solutions in Salesforce. Customer service professionals can search for available solutions in the solutions repository and can assign the appropriate solution to a case before updating the case status to closed.

We can searching for and install custom apps from AppExchange in order to further customize Salesforce to match our organization's requirements. AppExchange is similar to Google play app store and contains various types of apps or solutions. We can browse through these apps according to functionality or industry and can install the suitable app to our Salesforce instance. We can install an app from AppExchange in a sandbox to test the functionality before installing the same in a production environment.

An information system can transform processes in an organization only when the relevant employees in an company regularly use the system for their daily activities. The company can then monitor the expected gains in efficiency and effectiveness from using the system.

Agile change management and system deployment practices are essential to increase Salesforce adoption among users. Precise and relevant training tools can motivate sales and marketing professionals to track and perform their regular tasks from Salesforce. Similarly, companies can map performance ratings and incentives of users to the activities that are completed on Salesforce.

You can use Salesforce to manage your leads and sales pipeline in a strategic manner. You can initially use Salesforce as a consolidated platform to manage records and activities across sales, marketing and service teams. I wish you the very best as you continue to build your expertise and explore the various features in Salesforce.

www.ingramcontent.com/pod-product-compliance
Lightning Source LLC
Chambersburg PA
CBHW031238050326
40690CB00007B/855